Becoming a Learning Organization

D1525180

Becoming a Learning Organization

Beyond the Learning Curve

Joop Swieringa
André Wierdsma
Management Development Centre, Nijenrode,
The Netherlands School of Business

♦ **ADDISON-WESLEY PUBLISHING COMPANY**
Wokingham, England • Reading, Massachusetts • Menlo Park,
California • New York • Don Mills, Ontario • Amsterdam • Bonn
Sydney • Singapore • Tokyo • Madrid • San Juan • Milan • Paris
Mexico City • Seoul • Taipei

This book is in the Addison-Wesley Series on Organization Development.
Editors: Edgar H. Schein, Richard Beckhard

Translated by Logotechnics Ltd. (Sheffield – Zürich).
Typeset by Logotechnics Ltd. (Sheffield – Zürich) in Trump Medieval.
Text designed by Valerie O'Donnell.
Printed in Great Britain at the University Press, Cambridge.

First printed 1992.

ISBN 0–201–62753–1

British Library Cataloguing in Data Publication
A catalogue record for this book is available from the British Library.

Library of Congress Cataloging-in-Publication Data
A catalog record for this book is available from the Library of Congress.

Other Titles in the Organization Development Series

Total Quality: A User's Guide for Implementation
Dan Ciampa
1992 (54992)
Today's companies are required to be competitive not only with product quality, but with improved customer services, organizational excellence, competitive pricing and improved employee motivation. The challenge of achieving this Total Quality is addressed in this title, which offers clear and practical advice on how to implement a company-wide commitment to maximizing quality. It discusses both the managerial strategies and attitudes required for this effort and the ways in which all levels of the comapny must be involved to achieve it.

Parallel Learning Structures: Increasing Innovation in Bureaucracies
Gervase R. Bushe and A.B. Shani
1991 (52427)
Parallel learning structures are technostructural interventions that promote system-wide change in bureaucracies while retaining the advantages of bureaucratic design. This text serves as a resource of models and theories built around five cases of parallel learning structures that can help those who create and maintain them be more effective and successful. For those new to parallel learning structures, the text provides practical advice as to when and how to use them.

Managing in the New Team Environment: Skills, Tools, and Methods
Larry Hirschhorn
1991 (52503)
This text is designed to help manage the tensions and complexities that arise for managers seeking to guide employees in a team environment. Based on an interactive video course developed at IBM, the text takes managers step by step through the process of building a team and authorizing it to act while they learn to step back and delegate. Specific issues addressed are how to give a team structure, how to facilitate its basic processes, and how to acknowledge differences in relationships among team members and between the manager and individual team members.

Leading Business Teams: How Teams Can Use Technology and Group Process Tools to Enhance Performance
Robert Johansen, David Sibbett, Suzyn Benson, Alexia Martin, Robert Mittman, and Paul Saffo
1991 (52829)
What technology or tools should organization development people or team leaders have at their command, now and in the future? This text explores the intersection of technology and business teams, a new and largely uncharted area that goes by several labels, including 'groupware' a term that encompasses both electronic and nonelectronic tools for teams. This is the first book of its kind from the field describing what works for business teams and what does not.

The Conflict-Positive Organization: Stimulate Diversity and Create Unity
Dean Tjosvold
1991 (51485)
This book describes how managers and employees can use conflict to find common ground, solve problems, and strengthen morale and relationships. By showing how well-managed conflict invigorates and empowers teams and organizations, the text demonstrates how conflict is vital for a company's continuous improvement and increased competitive advantage.

Change by Design
Robert R. Blake, Jane Srygley Mouton, and Anne Adams McCanse
1989 (50748)
This book develops a systematic approach to organization development and provides readers with rich illustrations of coherent planned change. The book involves testing, examining, revising, and strengthening conceptual foundations in order to create sharper corporate focus and increased predictability of successful organization development.

Organization Development in Health Care
R. Wayne Boss
1989 (18364)
This is the first book to discuss the intricacies of the health care industry. The book explains the impact of OD in creating healthy and viable organizations in the health care sector. Through unique and innovative techniques, hospitals are able to reduce nursing turnover, thereby resolving the nursing shortage problem. The text also addresses how OD can improve such bottom-line variables as cash flow and net profits.

Self-Designing Organizations: Learning How to Create High Performance
Susan Albers Mohrman and Thomas G. Cummings
1989 (14603)
This book looks beyond traditional approaches to organizational transition, offering a strategy for developing organizations that enables them to learn not only how to adjust to the dynamic environment in which they exist, but also how to achieve a higher level of performance. This strategy assumes that change is a learning process: the goal is continually refined as organizational members learn how to function more effectively and respond to dynamic conditions in their environment.

Power and Organization Development: Mobilizing Power to Implement Change
Larry E. Greiner and Virginia E. Schein
1988 (12185)
This book forges an important collaborative approach between two opposing and often contradictory approaches to

management: OD practitioners who espouse a 'more humane' workplace without understanding the political realities of getting things done, and practicing managers who feel comfortable with power but overlook the role of human potential in contributing to positive results.

Designing Organizations for High Performance
David P. Hanna
1988 (12693)
This book is the first to give insight into the actual processes you can use to translate organizational concepts into bottom-line improvements. Hanna's 'how-to' approach shows not only the successful methods of intervention, but also the plans behind them and the corresponding results.

Process Consultation, Volume I: Its Role in Organization Development, Second Edition
Edgar H. Schein
1988 (06736)
How can a situation be influenced in the workplace without the direct use of power or formal authority? This book presents the core theoretical foundations and basic prescriptions for effective management.

Organizational Transitions: Managing Complex Change, Second Edition
Richard Beckhard and Reuben T. Harris
1987 (10887)
This book discusses the choices involved in developing a management system appropriate to the 'transition state'. It also discusses commitment to change, organizational culture, and increasing and maintaining productivity, creativity, and innovation.

Organization Development: A Normative View
W. Warner Burke
1987 (10697)
This book concisely describes and defines the theories and practices of organization development and also looks at organization development as change in an organization's culture. It is a useful guide to the field of organization development and is invaluable

to managers, executives, practitioners and anyone desiring an excellent overview of this multifaceted field.

Team Building: Issues and Alternatives, Second Edition
William G. Dyer
1987 (18037)
Through the use of the techniques and procedures described in this book, managers and consultants can effectively prepare, apply, and follow up on the human processes affecting the productive functioning of teams.

The Technology Connection: Strategy and Change in the Information Age
Marc S. Gerstein
1987 (12188)
This is a book that guides managers and consultants through crucial decisions about the use of technology for increasing effectiveness and competitive advantage. It provides a useful way to think about the relationship between information technology, business strategy, and the process of change in organizations.

Stream Analysis: A Powerful Way to Diagnose and Manage Organizational Change
Jerry I. Porras
1987 (05693)
Drawing on a conceptual framework that helps the reader to better understand organizations, this book shows how to diagnose failings in organizational functioning and how to plan a comprehensive set of actions needed to change the organization into a more effective system.

Process Consultation, Volume II: Lessons for Managers and Consultants
Edgar H. Schein
1987 (06744)
This book shows the viability of the process consultation model for working with human systems. Like Schein's first volume on process consultation, the second volume focuses on the moment-to-moment behavior of the manager or consultant rather than on the design of the OD program.

Managing Conflict: Interpersonal Dialogue and Third-Party Roles, Second Edition
Richard E. Walton
1987 (08859)
This book shows how to implement a dialogue approach to conflict management. It presents a framework for diagnosing recurring conflicts and suggests several basic options for controlling or resolving them.

Pay and Organization Development
Edward E. Lawler
1981 (03990)
This book examines the important role that reward systems play in organization development efforts. By combining examples and specific recommendations with conceptual material, it organizes the various topics and puts them into a total systems perspective. Specific pay approaches such as gainsharing, skill-based pay, and flexible benefits are discussed and their impact on productivity and the quality of work life is analyzed.

Work Redesign
J. Richard Hackman and Greg R. Oldham
1980 (02779)
This book is a comprehensive, clearly written study of work design as a strategy for personal and organizational change. Linking theory and practical technologies, it develops traditional and alternative approaches to work design that can benefit both individuals and organizations.

Organizational Dynamics: Diagnosis and Intervention
John P. Kotter
1978 (03890)
This book offers managers and OD specialists a powerful method of diagnosing organizational problems and of deciding when, where, and how to use (or not use) the diverse and growing number of organizational improvement tools that are available today. Comprehensive and fully integrated, the book includes many different concepts, research findings, and competing philosophies and provides specific examples of how to use the information to improve organizational functioning.

Career Dynamics: Matching Individual and Organizational Needs
Edgar H. Schein
1978 (06834)
This book studies the complexities of career development from both an individual and an organizational perspective. Changing needs throughout the adult life cycle, interaction of work and family, and integration of individual and organizational goals through human resource planning and development are all thoroughly explored.

Matrix
Stanley M. Davis and Paul Lawrence
1977 (01115)
This book defines and describes the matrix organization, a significant departure from the traditional 'one man–one boss' management system. The author notes that the tension between the need for independence (fostering innovation) and order (fostering efficiency) drives organizations to consider a matrix system. Among the issues addressed are reasons for using a matrix, methods for establishing one, the impact of the system on individuals, its hazards, and what types of organizations can use a matrix system.

Feedback and Organization Development: Using Data-Based Methods
David A. Nadler
1977 (05006)
This book addresses the use of data as a tool for organizational change. It attempts to bring together some of what is known from experience and research and to translate that knowledge into useful insights for those who are thinking about using data-based methods in organizations. The broad approach of the text is to treat a whole range of questions and issues considering the various uses of data as an organizational change tool.

Designing Complex Organizations
Jay Galbraith
1973 (02559)
This book attempts to present an analytical framework of the design of organizations, particularly of types of organizations that apply lateral decision processes or matrix forms. These

forms have become pervasive in all types of organizations, yet there is little systematic public knowledge about them. This book helps fill this gap.

Organization Development: Strategies and Models
Richard Beckhard
1969 (00448)
This book is written for managers, specialists, and students of management who are concerned with the planning of organization development programs to resolve the dilemmas brought about by a rapidly changing environment. Practiced teams of interdependent people must spend real time improving their methods of working, decision making, and communicating, and a planned, managed change is the first step toward effecting and maintaining these improvements.

Organization Development: Its Nature, Origins, and Prospects
Warren G. Bennis
1969 (00523)
This primer on OD is written with an eye toward the people in organizations who are interested in learning more about this educational strategy as well as for those practitioners and students of OD who may want a basic statement both to learn from and to argue with. The author treats the subject with a minimum of academic jargon and a maximum of concrete examples drawn from his own and others' experience.

Developing Organizations: Diagnosis and Action
Paul R. Lawrence and Jay W. Lorsch
1969 (04204)
This book is a personal statement of the authors' evolving experience, through research and consulting, in the work of developing organizations. The text presents the authors' overview of organization development, then proceeds to examine issues at each of three critical interfaces: the organization-environment interface, the group-group interface, and the individual-organization interface, including brief examples of work on each. The text concludes by pulling the themes together in a set of conclusions about organizational development issues as they present themselves to practicing managers.

About the Authors

Swieringa and Wierdsma have developed and run many in-company management development programmes at the Management Development Centre at Nijenrode. Course goals included:

- the implementation of a merger;
- the change-over from a functional to a divisional structure;
- the transition from product orientation to client/market orientation;
- the transition of a company from the pioneer phase to the organizational phase.

Dr Joop Swieringa (organizational adviser)
An economist by training and employed as such until 1978 in the health service. Assistant director of the Public Relations Office for Food and Nutrition from 1978 to 1981. Obtained doctorate during this period.

From 1981, employed at Nijenrode University, The Netherlands Business School; initially as senior lecturer in Organization and Management, subsequently as director of studies at the Management Development Centre. Directorship of the centre for one year.

Since 1 January 1989, associate director of the organizational advisory bureau, Veghtconsult.

Advised companies on matters such as: organization and organizational change; collaboration and leadership; management development; mission and strategy development and human resource management.

Fascinated by situations in which people collectively do what none of them wishes.

Drs André F. M. Wierdsma (Organizational psychologist)
Studied business administration at Nijenrode University and organizational and clinical psychology at the Free University. Employed since 1978 at Nijenrode University as Senior Lecturer in Management and Organization and director Executive MBA programme. Since 1981, employed at the Management Development Centre in Nijenrode. Teaching and publications in the field of (intercultural) communication and decision-making processes, organizational behaviour, management and change. Worked as visiting professor at the graduate School of Management at the University of Oregon in Eugene (Summer 1985) and for periods of two months in Beijing (PRC) at the China EEC Management Institute (CEMI) in the MBA programme (1986, 1988 and 1990) and for Executive training courses in 1991 and 1992.

Special interests in the influence of (international) culture on the theory and practice of management, organizing and change processes.

Foreword

The Addison-Wesley Series on Organization Development originated in the late 1960s when a number of us recognized that the growing field of 'OD' was not well understood or well defined. We also recognized that there was no one OD philosophy, and hence one could not at that time write a textbook on the theory and practice of OD, but one could make clear what various practitioners were doing under that label. So the original six books launched what has become a continuing enterprise, the essence of which was to allow different authors to speak for themselves instead of trying to summarize under one umbrella what was obviously a rapidly growing and highly diverse field.

By the early 1980s the series included nineteen titles. OD was growing by leaps and bounds, and it was expanding into all kinds of organizational areas and technologies of intervention. By this time, many textbooks existed as well that tried to capture the core concepts of this field, but we felt that diversity and innovation were still the more salient aspects of OD.

Now as we move into the 1990s our series includes twenty-eight titles, and we are beginning to see some real convergence in the underlying assumptions of OD. As we observe how different professionals working in different kinds of organizations and occupational communities make their case, we see we are still far from having a single 'theory' of organization development. Yet, a set of common assumptions is surfacing. We are beginning to see patterns in what works and what does not work, and we are becoming more articulate about these patterns. We are also seeing the field connecting to broader themes in the organizational sciences, and new theories and theories of practice are being presented in such areas as conflict resolution, group dynamics, and the process of change in relationship to culture. The new titles in the series address current themes directly: Ciampa's *Total Quality*, for example, addresses the challenge of creating a climate where employees continuously improve their ability to provide products and services that customers will find of particular value; Johansen et al.'s *Leading Business Teams* draws the link between OD skills and emerging electronic tools for teams; Tjosvold's *The Conflict-Positive Organization* connects to a whole research tradition on the dynamics of collaboration, competition, and conflict; Hirschhorn's *Managing in the New Team Environment* contains important links to psychoanalytic group theory; and Bushe and Shani's *Parallel Learning Structures* presents a seminal theory of large–scale organization change based on the institution of parallel systems as change agents.

As editors we have not dictated these connections, nor have we asked authors to work on higher-order concepts and theories. It is just happening, and it is a welcome turn of events. Perhaps it is an indication that OD may be reaching a period of consolidation and integration. We hope that we can contribute to this trend with future volumes.

Cambridge, Massachusetts   Richard H. Beckhard
New York, New York   Edgar H. Schein

Foreword

In recent years, the term 'learning organization' has appeared more and more frequently in management periodicals and books, seminars and conferences. In these contexts the phrase is always connected with the ever increasing speed of technological, economic and social changes which our organizations are facing. It is no longer adequate for organizations to react to them; they must anticipate them. It is not enough to maintain the present position; it is a question of being in the forefront of development. This places a demand on those organizations which have the ability to undertake a continuous process of change. The ability to change cannot, however, be bought; it must be learned by an organization. Learning to learn is the subject of this book.

The book derives its great strength from having been written from practical experience. The views, concepts and theories dealt with in the book arise from questions with which the authors have worked in past years.

We were one of these organizations, struggling with problems of integration following a merger. In tackling them with the help of the authors we took our first steps on the road towards becoming a learning organization.

What was most striking in this period of intense collaboration was the authors' great commitment. A commitment which guarantees a thorough treatment of this subject.

For these reasons I thoroughly recommend this book.

Drs J. F. M. Peters,
Chairman of the Board of Management, Aegon.

Preface

In recent years, we have accommodated about 500 managers in the Arena. (Arena is the name of the most important conference hall at the Management Development Centre at Nijenrode University, The Netherlands Business School.) They were, for the most part, managers from Aegon, Gist-brocades, IBM, OLM, Otra, PTT-Telecom and Shell and other companies. Companies which faced the need to adapt to the changing demands of their environment. For managers, this has meant that they were considered as educators in a process of change which was actually also a learning process for them. Our role was to help them in this process, which we shared with them as partners. Together, we experienced not only the enrichment, but also the painfulness of learning. It is, therefore, primarily to these managers that we owe a debt of gratitude. We should also like to thank all those who have helped us with the preparation of this book, especially Hans Mak, Director of Veghtconsult, who gave us the decisive impetus to begin; also, our colleagues at the MDC, who were always ready to put our ideas, opinions, concepts and methods to the test in lively discussion. A special word of thanks to Professor Paul Koopman, Professor Gerard Bomers, ir Luc Hoebeke, ir Edjan van Diest and once again, Drs Hans Mak, who have given our manuscript the benefit of their scrutiny and provided useful, constructive criticism. We extend further thanks to Marieke Paymans, Marjon van Tol-Steefkerk and Petra van Dijk of Veghtconsult who put the manuscript into a form in which it could be sent to the publisher.

We have sought publication for this book, emboldened by the belief that we have new thoughts and perceptions to offer. At the same time, however, we realize that our contribution is merely one brick in a construction whose foundations were laid by others. They are referred to in the bibliography, in which we have included the publications which have inspired us.

A final word of gratitude is reserved for our colleague Pieter van Gelein Vitringa, who died in an accident in 1986. It was he who inspired our quest for the fundamental ideas of collective learning and education. Pieter, thanks again.

Joop Swieringa and André Wierdsma
Breukelen, August 1992.

Contents

| Contents |

Introduction

> More time is wasted in educational programmes
> than through idleness.

This book is about *organizational change*. Our basic premise is that an organization can only be said to have changed when the people who work within it behave differently. Consequently this book is about learning, because we see learning as: *the changing of behaviour.*

The book is concerned with *learning* *by* *collectives*: organizations or parts of organizations. A central idea is that the ability of a group is more, and unfortunately sometimes also less, than the individuals of the collective. Ultimately, the book is concerned with *education* by which we mean helping to learn. In short, this is a book about facilitating organizational change.

The above, in a nutshell, is what the book is about. It is the result of reflecting on more than ten years' experience as educators in different management development programmes at the Management Development Centre (MDC) at Nijenrode University, The Netherlands Business School.

The MDC is a training institute which, since its foundation in 1981, has been devoted to the development and implementation of an entirely new sort of management development programme. So new that at first practically nobody – neither we nor the businesses in question – knew the precise implications of this sort of programme. Only now, ten years later, do we feel sufficiently confident about the subject to publish our experiences of it. We are, however, only too aware of the fact that we are writing about a subject on which the last word is as yet far from being spoken.

Up to the beginning of the 1980s, the only kind of conscious training of a company's own managers consisted almost exclusively in sending individual managers to what were known as management or executive development programmes. In the Netherlands these were offered by De Baak; and elsewhere, by business schools such as Harvard, Insead, IMI and IMEDE. These courses were specifically targeted at increasing insight into business administration. Managers were also sent to specific training courses to acquire skills in decision-making, communication, negotiation and conflict management.

Two important and not necessarily conscious basic assumptions underlay this practice. The first assumption was that there was such a thing as 'the one best way of management': a best way which could clearly be learned in colleges. The second assumption was that when the skills of individual *managers* were increased, this would automatically lead to better functioning of *management* and better still of the whole *organization*.

At the beginning of the 1980s, the realization that these assumptions were not correct began to emerge. Apparently, there was no such thing as the best way to manage. What was good for one business was not necessarily good for another. Also, the assumption that having skilled managers automatically leads to skilled management did not seem to follow. One was constantly confronted with the fact that individually skilled managers could be absolutely unskilled at working collectively.

At roughly the same time, many organizations and especially larger bureaucracies were faced with more and more radical changes in their environment, changes which could no longer be addressed by traditional methods. Until the 1980s the classical response to changes in the environment was reorganization. First of all a new strategy was developed, and then a corresponding new structure was subsequently implemented or, to put it more plainly, imposed from above, on the assumption that people would in time automatically function according to this new strategy and structure. This assumption, too, seemed less and less valid. Doubts about the effectiveness of strategy and structure as instruments of organizational change were making themselves increasingly apparent. They were instruments which only had an effect in the long term and furthermore, by definition, they led to stability. This, when many businesses were currently facing the challenge of creating an organization which was to be capable of rapid and continuous adaptation to the changing environment. It is gradually becoming evident that this kind of adaptability cannot be manufactured primarily by means of strategies, structures and everything associated with them (such as regulations, rules and procedures), but rather with the help of people themselves. People must create and adapt the organization, not vice versa. This can only be achieved through learning; starting with those who play the key role in the organization: the managers.

Against this background, the demand for a different kind of educational course arose in the 1980s, especially for managers. At that time nobody knew exactly what this type of course should consist of or how it should be designed. The clearest proof of this is the wide variety of differing, often meaningless names for this type of course. *Tailor-made courses*, for example, is a name which emphasizes that it is not a matter of standard programmes developed by an educational institute according to its own ideas, to which companies subscribe, but a course specially designed for the company concerned. Another name is *in-company education*, which is intended to indicate a programme exclusively designed for the staff (managers) within the company itself.

The two above-mentioned terms became quickly established. However, we feel that they have scarcely touched on the essential qualities required of this sort of course. Around 1987 the term *collective (management) courses* arose, with the implication of learning together, learning from each other. Towards the end of the 1980s more precise terms were coined such as 'education for organizational change'. In this book we will speak of *organizational education courses*.

We have divided the book into three parts. Part One is the conceptual part, where we develop the concepts of and closely define learning and education, especially organizational learning.

In Part Two we describe various types of organization according to how they learn.

Finally, Part Three is concerned with the education of organizations, in particular with what we call organizational education courses.

The key question which runs like a common thread through this book is: *how can organizations develop into learning organizations?* It is a question about organizations within which people learn through working together and work together through learning; organizations which are capable of sustaining their own development. What these organizations actually look like, only the future can tell. It is certain that they will be wholly different from those with which we are familiar. It is our conviction that classical organization theory, as it has evolved over the last hundred years, is standing on the threshold of a new age. In the final section we explain why this is the case.

It is not our intention to present a scientific treatise in this book, but rather to offer the benefit of our practical experience to managers, organization consultants, educators and indeed anyone who is concerned with the changing of organizations.

Part One
Basic Concepts

The aim of this book is to describe, and thereby make accessible, what we have learned in the last ten years about the learning and education of organizations. We describe our own perceptions and experiences as consultants and educators, our analyses of and our reflections on these experiences. We wish to do this in a systematic way so that our description rises above the level of casuistry. It will therefore first be necessary, in Part One, to introduce and discuss a number of basic concepts pertaining to organizations (Chapter Two), learning (Chapter Three) and education (Chapter Four) – the three main themes of this book. Starting from these basic concepts we develop, in Chapter Five, what we understand by collective learning or organizational learning.

The basic terms we introduce denote concepts we have found useful and valuable throughout the course of our professional lives.

Part One begins with a chapter on collective behaviour in organizations which in future we shall call organizational behaviour. In this chapter we describe how collective behaviour emerges and develops in an organization. We do this by outlining the development of a business.

On the Development of Organizational Behaviour

> In the beginning, an organization is an entrepreneur.

1.1 THE BUSINESS IN THE EARLY STAGES

At the basis of every business is the founder. This is usually a person with a strong drive to provide and market a product or service. The founder employs people who share this goal and drive and who are skilled in the jobs which have to be done. On the basis of the demands of the work (on the one hand), and the skills of the employees (on the other hand), tasks are divided up by mutual agreement. In this context the task determines what has to be done, ability determines who should do it and the founder determines how that should be accomplished and, in particular, how they are to cooperate. The founder determines both the rules of the game and the way in which the game must be played within them. The situation is comparable to a game of chess between a grand master and a beginner. One-sidedly, but within the rules of the game, the grand master determines the course of action during the play.

In this way a degree of homogeneity and predictability arises in the behaviour of the staff, based on both the demands of the work and the founder's ideas. This *collective* element in the behaviour of individuals is what we call *organizational behaviour*.

In the early stages of a business, the founder exercises a dominant, cohesive influence in the organization, giving direction and reducing uncertainty. This results in a feeling of familiarity (this is my club), direction and clarity, and saves time spent on mutually working out standards. Behaviour becomes predictable, makes mutual agreement easy and results in effective cooperation.

Once the staff have acquired a feel for the founder's views, values and preferences, their behaviour is no longer guided solely by their own judgement, but also by what they think is expected of them. Especially in matters which are important to the founder, they will tend to be led by their perception of what the founder wants to hear rather than their own beliefs.

1.2 THE GROWING BUSINESS

In the course of time the business will begin to grow. Inevitable expansion and changes of personnel gradually give rise to differences between established old hands and newcomers. The principal difference is that the original staff still know or apprehend what the founder's motives, preferences and ideas were which lie behind the rules. In this way they become the 'elite group'. The newcomers, however, are able to perceive only the rules and the game. They get a feel for the game, firstly, by copying the old hands and secondly because they get a rap across the knuckles if they play badly.

As growth continues the founder acquires an assistant who takes on responsibility for much of the time-consuming ground work. This assistant in turn gets another assistant and so on, leading to staff departments. Their function is to take care of the time-consuming groundwork in preparing proposals so the 'boss' can concentrate on decision-making. The frequency with which the 'boss' needs to be consulted is reduced by the development of rules and procedures by the departments. Through these rules and procedures the way the work is handled is formalized.

As the organization continues to grow the founder is forced to delegate coordinating roles to other members of staff, which results in the formation of middle management. An *organizational structure* takes shape, within which authorities and accountabilities are determined and lines of reporting are established. Agreements are formed on the handling of flows of cash and goods, procedures for communication and decision-making and guidelines for reporting and appraisal. In short, *management systems* arise.

The founder's influence on the behaviour of employees becomes more and more indirect. The founder's preferences, visions and ideas are expressed in the choice of structures, systems and corporate strategy. His (her) vision congeals as it were in these choices. The founder's direct influence is increasingly limited to the elite, who have become the bearers of the opinions, values and norms. A *company culture* develops.

1.3 THE ESTABLISHED BUSINESS

The founder is succeeded by a manager. The business takes on all the characteristics of a bureaucracy: hierarchical stratification, many influential staff departments, standardization of input and output norms, the skills of the people and the work processes. Structure, systems and strategy control the organizational behaviour of employees to an ever greater extent. The founder's influence, transmitted via the cultural component, is now only heard via stories and anecdotes which have meanwhile become myths. The question of who decides what, and who must do what and how, can no longer be answered unequivocally. Many 'players' have joined the game: line managers, members of staff and employees, all of whom have their influence.

In terms of the chess game, the situation is no longer a match between a grand master and a beginner, but is a question of equally matched players. The course of the game is not determined by one person alone, and a game evolves which is influenced by several players. The game begins to have dynamics of its own. The game and the rules of the game become the result of complex, implicit and explicit interaction processes between people, each of whom has personal views and principles about working together. These are all people who, on the basis of judgements and prejudices, appraisals of feasibility, need for power and ideological motives, make themselves more or less strong in defence of their ideas on the subject. Organizational reality cannot be taken for granted, it must be seen as the result of negotiation.

Members of the organization all play the game, but their

influence is by no means equal. There are the elite, who, because of their position and involvement, have more power than others over the nature of the game, how it is to be played and to what purpose. They determine the identity of the organization and consequently take over the key role, once occupied by the founder. They transmit the culture and guard the boundaries of the organization.

1.4 THE CENTRAL QUESTION

The intention behind this simplified description of the development of organizations was to illustrate how organizational behaviour evolves and continues to evolve.

By the term *organizational behaviour* we mean *the collective elements and patterns in the behaviour of people working in an organization.*

Organizational behaviour arises through the establishment of rules about working together and about how the game must be played within these rules.

In the early stages of a business the rules are laid down by the founder, who also supervises that employees live up to them. As the organization grows, this function is taken over more and more by strategy, structure, systems and culture. However, the rules thereby become more complex, and the way they are formed becomes less transparent.

The more complex the rules and the less transparent their formation, the harder they are to change. Organizational behaviour also becomes more difficult to change, and this is the central question of this book.

What is to be done when the organizational behaviour developed in the course of time ceases to correspond to the demands of the situation or of the members of the organization? It is customary to try changing the rules, but the older the organization, the harder this becomes. Besides, changing the rules does not guarantee a change in organizational behaviour. In this book, we explore the possibilities of an opposite approach: try to change the behaviour first and the rules will change as a result of the process.

In short, initiate changes by starting a learning process: *collective learning.*

On Organizations

You can't shake hands with organizations.

2.1 THE TERM 'ORGANIZATION'

In theory as well as practice, the term 'organization' can be used in several senses. One speaks, for example, of Philips, Johnson Ltd, the local football team or the marketing department as 'organizations'. These are instances of the *institutional* sense of the term, referring to a concrete association of people working together.

Alternatively, we can speak of the organization of Philips or of Johnson Ltd, meaning for example the way in which tasks within the company, the club, or the department are distributed. This is an example of the *instrumental* sense of the term 'organization'. In this book we will be dealing with both senses. The meaning will usually be evident from the context. In this chapter, we are concerned with the instrumental sense of organization; organization as the instrument which regulates organizational behaviour.

There are many definitions and descriptions of the instrumental concept of organization. Often an attempt is made to describe the different components of which the instrumentality consists. We also implicitly used this approach in the previous chapter when we distinguished four components within the concept of organization: strategy, structure, culture and systems.

By *strategy* we mean the goals of the organization and the ways in which it seeks to realize them.

Structure means the division and grouping of tasks, authorities and responsibilities; structure determines the position of and relationship between members of the organization.

Systems mean the conditions and agreements relating to the manner in which processes (information, communication and decision-making) and flows (cash and goods) proceed.

Finally, *culture* can be defined as the combined sum of the individual opinions, shared values and norms of the members of the organization.

We realize only too well that by introducing the concepts of strategy, structure, systems and culture and by way in which we have defined the concepts, we have provided fuel for many pages of discussion. In the Introduction we made it clear that we did not wish to succumb to this temptation. We will settle for a few brief remarks.

The choice and definition of the four terms is largely pragmatic: it is at present, both in theory and in practice, one of the most usual ways of describing organizations (in the instrumental sense), especially where a description of organizational changes is involved. By this we understand the changes to be in one or more of these components. If a change in one component is to be effective, it will nearly always require changes in the other components.

Strategy, structure, culture and systems are therefore four separate components which, though interconnected, are yet distinct from each other. Together, they constitute the concept of organization in the instrumental sense. This kind of definition deviates from those writers, for example, who see the structure of an organization as an aspect of culture, in other words, who use interlocking concepts. However, anyone who reflects at length on the implications of the definitions will discover that the concepts alone, from the standpoint of mutual demarcation, raise the necessary questions. For example, the choice of a certain structure is often a choice which is to a large extent determined by explicitly or implicitly held views and values, that is, by elements of culture. Conversely, opinions, values and norms also develop within the framework of the realization of shared goals; an element of the concept strategy.

These examples illustrate the close connection between the components and their reciprocal interaction, which results in circular causality loops; one factor being influenced by another and in its turn influencing the first. The question as to which component is most influential is of less interest than understanding the pattern of reciprocal influences.

2.2 PRINCIPLES, INSIGHTS AND RULES

As far as this book is concerned it is not so important to understand exactly what strategy, structure, systems and culture *are*, but what they *do*; what effects they have. Well, they control organizational behaviour. They state, describe, determine, prescribe or dictate what kind of organizational behaviour is desired. Which of the verbs are most to the fore depends on the type of organization, as we shall see later. The behaviour-controlling function of the said concepts can be expressed through the distinction, essential for our book, between rules, insights and principles.

We have already referred to rules in the preceding chapter. *The minimum requirement to be able to speak of an organization is a set of rules.* That is the barest definition of organization in the instrumental sense.

In the broadest and most neutral sense of the word, rules are all explicit and implicit instructions affecting the desired behaviour. Explicit instructions can be laid down in writing in manuals, diagrams, methods, job descriptions, authorizations, procedures and regulations, or can be imparted or agreed orally. Implicit instructions can be deduced from rituals, symbols, anecdotes and not least from non-verbal behaviour such as gestures, attitudes and silences.

Rules indicate *how* the organization – in the institutional sense – should behave.

These rules are based to a greater or lesser extent on *insights* into what a good organization is, can do and how it should be run: the founder's insights about running the business in its early stages and later on insights from the elite in the established company. By insights we mean the more or less refined and reliable explicit, logical arguments, theories, concepts and opinions about purchasing, sales and production, about decision-making and communication, budgeting and administration. In short, insights into how to run a business; how to organize and how to manage cooperation between people to produce goods or offer services in the market.

The function of these insights is to (be able to) *explain* and *understand* existing rules or to (be able to) develop adequate new rules.

The third category consists of what we call *principles*; to a greater or lesser extent shared assumptions and core beliefs indicating the sort of business we *wish* to be. Principles constitute the essence of the business: the identity of the organization in the institutional sense. Some writers call it ideology; Lievegoed speaks of the 'policy system'; for Schein this is precisely the culture of the organization itself, and Hasper describes it as the individuality of the organization. Principles are the views and assumptions which transcend speech, logic and theory and cannot therefore be put up for discussion. Principles determine the 'taken for granted' reality, the definition of reality that should be accepted without protest by those employees who wish to be loyal to the organization. In the company in its early stages, they are manifested in the personality of the founder, and in established companies they are carried by the personalities of those who represent the culture, as self-evident truths. The function of these principles is to establish and maintain mutual cohesion between the prevalent insights and rules. Insights provide meaning and significance for principles and rules.

We can summarize by saying that organization consists of a combination of rules, insights and principles. Rules formulate what we *must do and are allowed to do*; insights represent what we *know and understand*; principles represent what we *are or wish to be*.

2.3 THE RELATIONSHIP BETWEEN RULES, INSIGHTS AND PRINCIPLES

As is already clear from the order in which we have spoken about rules, insights and principles, we see at different levels with respect to organizational behaviour. We have represented this diagrammatically in Figure 1. We fully realize that with such a diagram, while bringing order into complex reality, we are thereby at the same time simplifying it to a great extent.

The rules are closest to organizational behaviour; they must be present in every case in order to be able to speak of an organization. However, at the same time an organization is for many of its members, especially those lower in the organization, often no more than a system of rules, whose logic is only partly understood and which is therefore only partially accepted.

Rules have a direct influence on the behaviour of the members. They determine the range of what people are allowed to do and must do.

Although insights can have a direct influence on behaviour – people often do act differently, simply because they know more or understand more – their influence is channelled to a great extent via the rules. The influence of insights is thus largely indirect. This, in itself, means that insights are less easily influenced by the members. Furthermore, insights are more difficult to discuss than rules, because this demands more knowledge and requires more time, energy and commitment. The consequences of a change in insight are further reaching and can have repercussions on other insights, standpoints and interests.

The same is true of principles but to an even greater extent, since our *will* is now involved. Values are much more involved in questions of will than with the preceding two categories. This makes these questions perhaps the most difficult of all to discuss within an organization. It is easier to arrive at a

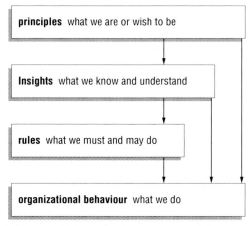

Figure 1 The relationship between rules, insights and principles.

compromise over the effects of values than over the initial principles themselves. The discussion is also often only the preserve of the dominant elite which sees itself as the guardian of the identity and boundaries of the organization. We have not discussed the influence of behaviour on rules, insights and principles here. It is obvious that they do not develop in a 'vacuum'. The famous sentence by Weick (1979) 'how can I know what I think, before I have seen what I have done' summarizes the impact of behaviour on our thinking.

This model is illuminating, but as we pointed out before, it is also a simplification. In practice, distinctions of this kind are often not so easy to draw. Furthermore, what counts as a rule in one organization (for example, 'do not exceed your own limits'), is a principle in another organization. We can also see that with time, rules such as 'make a good job of it', or insights such as 'matrix structures give rise to problems with accountabilities', have been elevated to principles in the sense of 'mistakes are not allowed and matrix structures are no good'. Movement in the other direction also occurs.

2.4 ORGANIZATIONAL IMAGES

In terms of function it is not important whether rules, insights and principles are implicit or explicit; in both cases, they contribute to the controlling of behaviour. However, as far as learning is concerned, the extent to which rules, insights and principles are implicit or explicit is of great importance. Learning processes within organizations where a great deal remains implicit and where rules, insights and principles have largely to be inferred from actually demonstrated behaviour are very different from learning processes in organizations where these are as far as possible made explicit.

Even with explicit rules, insights and principles, an intermediate, interpretative stage is needed for the process of recognizing and understanding them; a phase in which one asks oneself how the rules are to be understood, what significance is to be attached to them and how they are experienced and acted out. The decisive feature for the influence on behaviour is not the rules 'as such' but the image, the perception or the interpretation given to them. Clearly not all aspects of organization are equally subject to interpretation. Systems based on technology are, for example, seen much more as a fact than culture, a component which always leads to many different interpretations. Interpretative processes are always there. There is no 'objective' reality outside of us waiting to be discovered.

A significant part of organization is thus in people's minds, and it is the images of reality stored up in these minds which determine behaviour. This applies to images of the content as well as the form of the rules, insights and principles. It can happen that exactly the same rule is seen as a regulation or command by most people in one organization, while in another this is understood as an agreement. In one case the same rule has a completely different effect on people's action from that in the other case. The effect is not determined by precisely what is contained in the rule or by the intention behind it, but by how the rule is interpreted. One reason for the occurrence of discrepancies between desired and actual behaviour in an organization is that the images people have of their organization are always incomplete and often quite different. A significant component of organizational learning consists then in the mutual exchange and complementing of the images one has of the work processes, cooperation between each other and one's own actions.

2.5 ORGANIZATION AS A CONSTRUCTION OR SYSTEM

There has been a battle for years now between the exponents of (inter)action theory and the exponents of systems theory. The first faction sees an organization as the resultant of a shared process of giving, meaning the result of interaction between the members: social construction. The second faction sees organization as a system with its own principles and regularities, of which people merely form one of many elements. Both factions try their hardest to convince each other of the truth of their own definition. Adherents of the interaction theory in particular should see that this is senseless. In any organizational change it is far more important to understand how the perception or interpretation of the organization influences behaviour, than what the organization 'really' is. An organization is both a construction and a system. Organizations are developed by people in mutual interaction with each other and through the exchange of images. At the same time, however, mechanisms on a social level give the developed construction a life of its own, so that it removes itself to a greater or lesser extent from the direct influence of the individual members. The extent to which this is true depends again on how people experience or perceive their own organization; as a system or a construction. This can vary considerably from business to business. One effect which can arise is that an organization which is widely perceived as a system by its members can, as a result, develop more and more elements which actually make it into an organization with a system; a self-fulfilling prophecy.

It is this difference in the experiencing and perception by members of their own organization which largely determines what and how an organization learns.

2.6 ORGANIZATION, MANAGEMENT AND LEADERSHIP

We will conclude this chapter with a few remarks about the relationship between organization, management and leadership. As in the case of organization there are many definitions of the terms 'management' and 'manager'. One key element in nearly all definitions is that the function of management is: *to direct people towards the desired behaviour.*

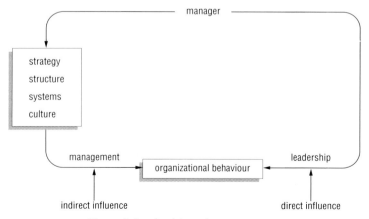

Figure 2 Leadership and management.

This can be achieved in two ways, directly or indirectly. *Direct* means through direct interaction with the employee; by instructing, persuading, coaching, advising, and motivating. This is what we usually describe as *leadership*. *Indirect* means through the development of an effective organization, including strategy, structure, culture and systems. We will refer to this as *management*. By this definition, management is indirect leadership.

According to this definition of management, an organization in the instrumental sense is a series of instruments: strategy, structure, culture and systems. These instruments are used by management in order to control behaviour, so that it fulfils the demands of the external environment. This approach is compatible with a business in which organization is largely seen as a system, and where the function of management is to design and lead a system. The majority of books on 'management and organization' are written with this approach in mind. However, if management is seen as largely a social construction, then managers are primarily leaders; people who make choices concerning the positioning of the company within its environment, who filter signals and play an innovative, stimulating and decisive role in the process of organizing.

On Learning

> Someone who only knows what he has learned
> and not how he learned it, still has a lot to learn.

3.1 LEARNING IS BEHAVIOURAL CHANGE

Learning is the *changing of behaviour*. The goal of this change in behaviour is to arrive at a form of behaviour which corresponds better to the goals of the learner; in other words, behaviour that is more effective. We call this *competence.*

Leaving aside the many nuances and side issues which could be raised, this is a generally accepted definition of learning, not only in theory but certainly also in everyday practice. We thus speak of learning to walk, cycle, program, keep accounts, cooperate, negotiate, give the lead and so forth. It is also a definition which has a particular appeal for managers. This makes it all the more curious that management educators (lecturers, course designers, organisers of seminars and so on) in general prefer a much more restricted definition. If one attends the lectures, seminars and courses in this field, one often gains the impression that learning is equated exclusively with increasing knowledge; and education with imparting this body of knowledge.

We should make it clear that it is not our intention to undermine the relevance of *knowledge* and *insight*, which can scarcely be overestimated, but we are concerned that in many management and business courses, all the emphasis is on the imparting of knowledge and insights alone, while scarcely any or no consideration is given to the development of competence. Competence is not determined only by what people know or understand but also by what they can do (skills), what they have the *courage* and *will* to do and who they *are* (personality and attitude).

Perhaps this is one reason why in addition to management and business courses a circuit has arisen of management training (or 'doing courses') in the areas of communication, sales, decision-making and negotiation. However, these courses in their turn undervalue knowledge and insight. Management really requires an integration of knowledge, understanding and ability; an integration which also requires courage and commitment.

Knowing and understanding (knowledge and insight) are *necessary* but not in the least *sufficient* prerequisites of ability (skill). A clever person is not always a competent one. Even ability is not sufficient. You must also have the will and the courage to act. It is precisely this personal attitude which bridges the gap between knowledge and understanding on the one hand and ability on the other.

To sum up: what and how much people have learned manifests itself through demonstrated behaviour; not through what they know or their abilities, or even what they venture and desire, but what they actually do with the knowledge, insights, skills and attitude.

The goal of learning is still to improve the quality of someone's actions. The concept of quality of action will henceforth be termed *competence*. An evaluation of the effectiveness of a learning process is therefore commensurate with assessing the extent to which someone's competence has been increased. This is applicable to the learning of individuals; it likewise applies to the learning of organizations. In the case of organizations we can also speak of the degree of competence demonstrated through organizational behaviour.

3.2 CONSCIOUS LEARNING VERSUS UNCONSCIOUS LEARNING

Not only is learning often identified with the acquisition of knowledge and insights, it is also, and frequently by the same people, equated with conscious learning. A great deal of learning, however, takes place unconsciously.

In his book *The Silent Language*, Hall distinguishes three types of learning: informal learning, formal learning and technical learning.

Informal learning is learning by *imitation*: picking up other people's skills. It is probably the earliest form of learning. The baby learning to say 'daddy', to nod and shake its head, to wave its hands to say hello learns that by imitation. But also in later life this remains an important form of learning in which we imitate people whom we consider skilled, whom we admire or like, and avoid imitating those we think unskilled or whom we dislike. In this type of learning there are thus always other people who fulfil the function of role models. Others who, often without realizing it, help to learn and thereby fulfil the role of educators.

Formal learning is learning by means of *rewards* and *punishments* such as compliments, incentives or bonuses, or disapproval, reprimands, refusals or punishment. This, too, is a very early form of learning; most of us learned about table manners and politeness in this way. Here again, learning takes place via the reactions of others and it is again crucial how significant the other person is to the learner.

Both formal and informal learning generally involve learning processes which often take place *unconsciously* and are often called learning by experience. The rules of the game governing our interactive behaviour are often learned in early childhood through 'experience'. We often only realize later – sometimes only years later – that we have learned this; a realization that gives us new insight into what we have learned. On the other hand there are many things we have learned of which we remain unconscious throughout our lives. Who, for example, is aware of the norm which determines the distance people should keep from each other, or of the fact that one has learned this or how this has been learned? Besides this agreement, there is also a significant difference between formal and informal learning. Learning through imitation is associated far less with emotions than learning through rewards and punishments. The latter, however unconscious this learning process may be, always arouses emotions to a greater or lesser extent. Rewards lead to feelings of pleasure, happiness or contentment and punishments may bring reactions of frustration, sorrow or recalcitrance. These emotions often re-emerge when one becomes aware of the learning process.

Methodical learning, the technical learning according to Hall, is *conscious* learning: it is being consciously occupied with learning, which also means that it is a question of a consciously chosen learning method. One of these methods may still be imitation.

Imitation can thus, just like rewards and punishments, also be a form of conscious learning.

Any learning in which education (helping to learn) plays a part is, by definition, methodical, conscious learning, and therefore encompasses learning in classrooms, lecture halls, seminars and on courses. However, this also applies to learning via correspondence courses, instruction manuals and so on. Methodical learning can also take place on the shop floor or behind the desk or in conversation with one or more colleagues.

Conscious learning leads to a higher level of competence, in that it is additive and on-going. Because they know *what* they have learned and *how*, people can decide to correct the process or continue it. In other words, conscious learning helps to develop *learning potential*, the potential to control one's own learning. By contrast, unconscious learning is *repetitive*; imitating role models or repeating behaviour which is rewarded and avoiding that which is punished. There is no innovation or change in perspective: it is repetitive. It is always others who determine what is learned. An uncomfortable consequence of competence gained in this way is that it suddenly threatens to have less value when the system of reward or punishment is changed or when people who served as the role models go away.

To sum up: learning is often implicitly equated with conscious learning. However, much behaviour, collective behaviour in particular, is learned unconsciously, both formally and informally. It is for this reason that there are still so many organizations in which a great deal is learned, but whose learning potential is nevertheless very low.

3.3 CYCLIC LEARNING

The difference between conscious and unconscious learning is often identified with the difference between learning through education and learning through experience. It can be seen from staffing policies that some companies have a strong preference for people who have learned in the first way, and thus they recruit people predominantly on the basis of colleges and universities attended, while some companies scarcely take account of degrees, titles and the like and recruit people on the basis of their experience.

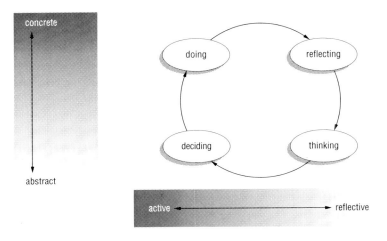

Figure 3 The Kolb learning cycle.

In fact the distinction here is quite senseless. Everyone knows that wide experience is no guarantee of wide knowledge, understanding or ability and therefore of competence. Whether and how much people learn from their experiences depends, not so much on what and how much they experience, but on what they do with what they experience. Many people merely live out their experience instead of learning from it. *Mutatis mutandis,* the same thing can be said of learning via education.

Kolb was one of several writers who put an end to this difference, precisely by building a bridge between these methods of learning. Interpreted somewhat freely, Kolb maintains that learning is a cyclic process: doing → reflecting → thinking → deciding → (re)doing (see Figure 3).

One gains experience through doing; reflecting is the meditating on this experience; thinking is the attempt to understand that experience by means of analysis and conceptualization; one then makes choices, decides on the next steps and then the cycle repeats itself. The circle recognizes two axes showing the poles around which learning takes place; one extends from *action* to *reflection,* the other from *concrete* to *abstract.*

According to this approach, learning is a never ending and constantly repeated process. It may be a matter of very short cycles of a few minutes, or extend to cycles of days or even years, depending on the level of the learning experience. Thus, directly after consulting with a client (doing), an organizational consultant may wonder how things went, what went wrong and what went well and what part he played in it (reflecting), examine what the reasons and causes were (thinking) and draw conclusions in preparation for the next meeting (deciding). This is a cycle which can be completed within a day. However, if we set about writing a book like this one, it is the result of reflection on and analysis of ten years of experience.

Kolb's approach has many attractive aspects. In the first place, Kolb does not make the mistake of equating learning with the acquisition of knowledge. Putting it more strongly, it was precisely his opposition to this idea which motivated him to design another learning model in which the acquisition of knowledge and insight is integrated with the development of skills and attitudes. His starting point is: what people have learned must be evident from what they do. This is why Kolb's viewpoint has been described as 'learning by experience' or 'learning by doing'. Kolb himself prefers to speak of problem-solving or *problem-oriented* learning. There is some justification for this, since problems represent both the motive and the vehicle for learning in his model. This is the second attractive point in his method of approach, which makes it directly relevant to the theme of this book. For in organizational learning, problems are also both the stimulus and the medium for learning. Thirdly, his model offers very concrete points to make use of in education, and we shall be coming back to this in the next chapter.

The central ideas of the Kolb model are that it considers that everyday activities can be a component of learning processes, and that it states how these often unconscious activity processes, in conjunction with thinking and deciding, can be raised to the level of conscious learning. That is the greatest advantage of this model, since, as has been said, conscious learning leads to a higher level of competence than unconscious learning.

3.4 SELF-KNOWLEDGE AND LEARNING POTENTIAL

Conscious learning, as we have stated, is a prerequisite for the development of learning potential. The source of it is learning who you are, both in other people's eyes and in your own. Greater self-knowledge leads to a greater learning potential.

In global terms three levels of self-knowledge can be distinguished (see Figure 4).

The first level is knowledge of what you *can do*; knowing what you can do if you want to have a reasonable chance of success or what is better avoided. It is a form of self-knowledge which prevents under- or over-estimation of your abilities. The second level is knowledge of what you *know*, and in particular, what you *understand*. Self-confidence is often based on this type of self-knowledge. The third level, which is likewise the core, concerns knowledge of who you *are* and *wish to be*. This level of knowledge forms the basis of your personality and identity.

The higher the level of self-knowledge, the greater the learning potential. People who have poor insight into what they can and cannot do tend to learn badly. If that is indeed the case and the underlying insight is lacking, learning is then restricted to learning by rote. If this understanding is present, but you do not know what you want, learning remains a directionless

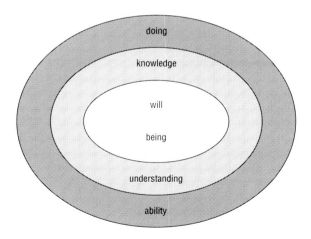

Figure 4 Self-knowledge.

activity. The more you know what you can do, what you understand and wish, the more you can determine your own learning goals, learning path and method of learning.

Increasing self-knowledge requires feedback on the demonstrated competence or incompetence. Your competence is not determined solely by the image you yourself have of it (self-image), but also by the image others have of it. Learning, and particularly the acquisition of self-knowledge, is therefore only possible through interaction. This is fundamental and at the same time paradoxical: through entering into relationships with others you learn your own uniqueness or identity. The mirror other people hold up, showing you how your actions have been received, gives you information which corrects and completes your self-image.

3.5 LEARNING TO LEARN

Learning potential is a concept that refers to the potential to learn, but in particular to the potential for learning to learn. This is sometimes called meta-learning or self-education. The potential for learning to learn requires a special kind of self-knowledge, namely knowing the way in which you are learning. Kolb calls this someone's learning style: whether you are a doer

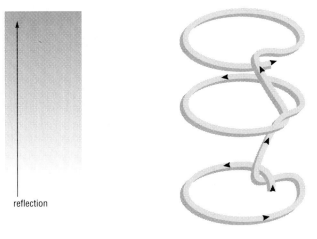

reflection

Figure 5 Learning to learn.

or reflecter or thinker or decider, with the attendant strengths and weaknesses. There is even more to it. It requires knowing your own blind spots, ways of reasoning and perceiving, assumptions, things which you would rather avoid or prefer to embark on.

The reflection phase has great significance in the learning process which leads to this self-knowledge. It is a phase which we in the western world are inclined to skip over too quickly. It is a question of reflecting on yourself in order to make close contact between you and your environment by asking yourself what the signals are that the environment gives out and drawing conclusions from them. The reflection phase is a phase where precise feedback from an outsider is necessary to set you on the right track.

Much research into creativity and innovative learning shows that it is precisely through reflection that both individuals and groups can make a 'leap' in their learning process. This leap demands the courage to accept that your own reality is not the only reality.

On Education

> University lecturers are often more
> interested in their own performance
> than their students' learning.

4.1 EDUCATION IS HELPING TO LEARN

Nobody can do your learning for you. That is something you must do for yourself at all times. The most that others can do is to *help with learning*, and this is what we call educating. In other words: education is the explicit initiation of a learning process and the conscious *interventions* in this learning process. This definition implies that education only has any point if the person being educated wants and needs to learn. Ultimately, therefore, the learner determines whether and what will be learned. An important consequence of this definition is that education must be based on a mutual *contract* between teacher and pupil.

For several decades a battle has been raging over the best method of education. It focuses on the question of how far the teacher should control the process of learning: to what extent the teacher should set the goals and strategies. The bones of contention are choices such as: directive or non-directive teaching; disciplined or free approaches; converging or diverging education.

In fact, this is no more than a methodological conflict in a world of thought where teachers teach students and education is synonymous with teaching and is not seen as helping to learn. However, if education is defined as helping to learn, much of this conflict appears quite unnecessary, as the fact has been recognized that learning can ultimately never be achieved by a teacher. The question of the required extent of teacher control can then simply be answered: it depends on the agreement or contract between teacher and 'pupil'. That may on the one hand be a contract in which the student agrees to the learning goals and strategies set down by the teacher, conforming therefore to a rather directive approach or else a contract in which the student states the kind of assistance expected from the teacher.

There are doubtless readers who could argue, with examples, that this definition is not tenable since learning can and does take place against the will. In other words: it is not so much that a value-free definition is given as that a normative standpoint has been formulated. This may be true, but if learning is not based on a mutual contract, then in our opinion it is no longer education, but more like patronization, in which case the learner is not being treated as an adult. The particular goal of this book is to discuss the learning and education of adults.

4.2 EDUCATION, TRAINING AND FORMING

Education has traditionally been divided into three parts: education in the narrower sense, training and forming. These concepts again and again give rise to misunderstanding. One of the most important reasons for this is that the concepts are used to refer to types of educational programmes as well as to types of educational intervention (see Section 4.3).

When referring to types of *educational programmes*, we understand the word 'education' in the narrower sense to mean programmes directed towards the acquisition of knowledge and understanding. Training courses are programmes directed towards the acquisition of skills. Forming courses are programmes directed towards the development of specific attitudes.

The implicit assumption underlying these three terms is that education, training and forming are different types of education, with the implication that skills can be learned without knowledge and insight. This distinction implicitly denies the definition of learning as the changing of behaviour; at least, it denies that each of these categories is a necessary but insufficient condition for learning, that is for changing behaviour.

The difference between the three categories has also not arisen from ideas about learning, but from a difference in methods of education in the wider sense. The fact that these three forms of education are independent is primarily a consequence of methodological specialization and professionalization within the world of education.

4.3 EDUCATION AS INTERVENTION

Using the terms introduced so far, it is possible to define the kind of help offered during the learning process. We have already defined learning as a cyclic process of doing, considering, thinking and deciding. Education then consists of making interventions in this process. These can be identified by the phase in the learning cycle. Thus we distinguish four, rather than three, sorts of intervention:

- help with *doing*, which can be described as *training*;
- help with *thinking*, described as *educating* in the narrower sense;
- help with *reflecting*, known as *forming*;
- help with *deciding*, usually called *consulting*.

In the cyclic view of learning, deciding is seen as an essential step in the learning process, but consulting is an educational

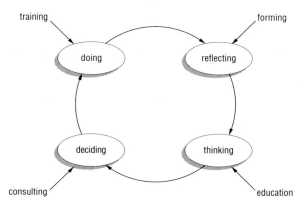

Figure 6 Interventions.

intervention; that is, consulting in the sense of helping with deciding, not consulting in the sense of working out solutions.

In all four types of intervention education always consists in providing:

- points of view, concepts and theories;
- methods and techniques;
- mirrors and feedback, and where it is a matter of problem-oriented learning;
- formulation of problems as case studies, games, exercises or role play.

The only difference between interventions is dictated by whether they are intended as help with doing, reflecting, thinking or deciding.

Theories and methods relating for example to the thinking phase aim to help with analysing, making connections and conceptualizing. Theories relating to the doing phase aim to help with testing, adaptation and execution. The same is true of problem formulation. A case may be presented with the aim of analysing a situation (thinking). The same case could be used for acting out the situation (doing), or for solving a problem (deciding).

The above can be expressed quite differently and, in the case of collective learning processes, more clearly, namely by making the distinction between content-specific, procedural and process-specific interventions.

Content-specific interventions are aimed at the content of learning. They consist in offering viewpoints, concepts and theories. Learning, particularly collective learning, takes place through interaction with others, and this is the process dimension of learning. There is a directly proportional relationship between content and process; the better the process, the better the content. *Process-specific* interventions are included in this interaction process, by means of confrontations, feedback and so on. The connection between content and process is made by procedures. *Procedural* interventions impinge upon all possible means relating to the approach; methods, techniques, rules and so on.

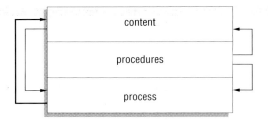

Figure 7 The relationship between content, process and procedures.

4.4 EDUCATION AS LEARNING TO LEARN

In Section 4.1, we introduced as a professional norm that in the education of adults, learning goals and strategies must be the result of a mutually agreed contract between teacher and student. This is the consequence of a viewpoint which holds that education is defined as helping to learn.

In concluding this chapter we wish to add a second professional norm, namely that educators should try to make themselves superfluous as soon as possible. Education, however it is conducted, must also aim to increase learning potential: the ability to learn how to learn. Teachers who fail to do this, create – perhaps unintentionally but they still do – a relationship of dependency between teacher and student, and this amounts in essence to not treating the learner as an adult.

On Organizational Learning

One plus one is sometimes one, sometimes two,
sometimes three.

5.1 ORGANIZATIONAL LEARNING IS COLLECTIVE LEARNING

By the term 'organizational learning' we mean the changing of organizational behaviour. The changing of organizational behaviour is a *collective learning process*. A learning process takes place in and through interaction with and between a number of people. Obviously, an organization can only learn because its individual members learn. Without individual learning there can be no question of organizational learning. On the other hand, an organization has not automatically learned when individuals within it have learned something. Individual learning is a *necessary* but *not a sufficient* condition for organizational learning.

An organization only learns if someone not only does the job better, but as a result of this other members of the organization operate differently. One can only speak of the learning of organizational behaviour when a change in the behaviour of one individual has an effect on the behaviour of others. In short, it must be a question of *mutual* behavioural change, and therefore mutual learning.

> The induction of new members of staff, sending managers on educational courses, or the introduction of job rotation results in individual learning. This does not automatically imply that the organization is also learning.
>
> A quality controller discovers that one shift is producing a higher proportion of substandard goods than the others. If the controller is content merely to increase watchfulness without telling the shift boss, or

does tell the boss, but the boss does not listen, then the controller has learned something, but the organization has not.

A departmental manager moves an employee who is not getting on with members of one team into another team, assuming that this will benefit the work of the team as well as of the employee. Even if this assumption proves to be correct the organization has not necessarily learned anything.

Collective learning is aimed at increasing the collective competence of the members of an organization or components of an organization.

It must be fairly obvious to anyone that collective competence is more than the sum of individual competences. How else is it possible for a football team, made up from the eleven best professional players in the Netherlands, to lose against the local Rijnsberg amateur footbal club? How else can you explain that a management team consisting of five top managers can still make completely wrong decisions?

It is much less widely known that collective competence also needs to be learned, and that this requires effort and time. The realities of industrial life provide daily examples which testify that people either cannot or will not understand this fact.

Two companies are about to merge, with the goal of total integration. Both are blessed with relatively competent management. Directly after the merger, however, decision-making, a management responsibility *par excellence*, falls into a state of almost total inertia. After six months, the Managing Director can contain himself no longer and decides on total reorganization.

In another case, a merger gives rise to intrigues, rumours and clandestine conflict. The initial reaction from the top is to suspend all forms of consultation. The next stage is diligent work on function and task descriptions. Thirdly, any possible informal consultations in coffee-breaks, staff canteens and so on, is prevented. The last stage, two years later, is to repudiate the merger formally.

A company transfers from a functional to a divisional structure. Management teams are formed for each division and decision-making is decentralized to a great extent to the level of the division. After six months, a quarter of the managers have been dismissed from their posts and a year later, decentralization has been almost totally abandoned.

Matrix organization is introduced into a department which had been organized on excessively functional lines. Before even nine months have elapsed, it is officially announced the the matrix does not appear to have fulfilled expectations.

For the first time in the forty year history of a small private company, a director is appointed who is not in the family, and who is not a co-owner. Three months later, he moves on, disappointed.

The common thread in each of these cases is that the people immediately started taking action, almost without any thought as to how people cooperate, and without giving each other the time to learn how to acquire collective competence.

5.2 COLLECTIVE LEARNING MEANS ORGANIZATIONAL CHANGE

In Chapter 1, we suggested that the salient feature of an organization – in the institutional sense – is that it is a matter of people cooperating: thinking things out together, taking decisions and carrying out activities. An organization manifests itself in the collective behaviour of its members, that is to say, in organizational behaviour. And ultimately in an organization there is only one question to be asked: are the members fulfilling relevant tasks to the best of their ability? Organizational change comes into play when one begins collectively to do things differently. In short, collective learning, the learning – and thus changing – of organizational behaviour is, in fact, equivalent to organizational change. By changing the behaviour of an organization, in the institutional sense, the organization also changes in the instrumental sense.

As we stated in Chapter 1, the minimum requirement to be able to speak about an organization is the existence of explicit or implicit rules relating to the desired organizational behaviour. So long as these rules lead to behaviour which delivers the desired results there is no need to change them. The organization does not need to learn. In fact, the only learning required is individual learning; learning to behave in accordance

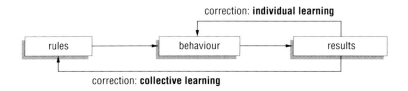

Figure 8a The concious learning of organizational behaviour.

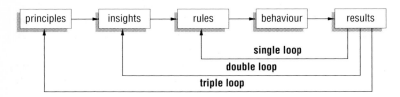

Figure 8b Collective learning loops.

with the rules. Introduction and induction programmes, specialist courses and individual skill training courses are almost always directed towards the individual learning of behaviour required by the organization.

Only when the rules no longer lead to behaviour which delivers the desired results does the need arise for learning at organizational level; that is to say, changing collective behaviour and changing the rules along with it, and that is exactly what happens with collective learning. At the very least a change in organizational behaviour entails that existing rules are changed or new ones developed. This does not necessarily imply changing rules in the objective sense, but rather in the sense in which they are interpreted and the images one has of them.

Such learning processes are frequently unconscious. Very many, more or less fixed, interaction patterns between staff themselves and between staff and their boss are learned unconsciously. None the less, implicit rules are developed in the process which often only become apparent when someone suddenly starts to deviate from them. For example, a manager returns from a leadership training course and tries to implement a completely new approach. If this fails, and the new behaviour is quickly eroded, no new organizational behaviour has been learned. However, if the staff more or less fit in with this new style of leadership, this indicates that collective learning has taken place, and that, however unconsciously, new rules have developed.

Conscious learning of organizational behaviour entails that it must be made mutually explicit which rules are concerned, how they are to be interpreted and what changes in them are considered necessary. 'Explicit' does not necessarily mean enshrined in writing. On the contrary, it often happens that the more firmly enshrined in writing rules are, the more implicit working with them becomes. Making rules explicit means telling each other what you are thinking, how situations are being interpreted and problems approached.

For organizational behaviour also it is a fact that conscious learning is of a higher quality than unconscious learning. By making the rules explicit, you can make clear to each other how each individual interprets the rules, how they are evaluated, what changes would be welcomed and what anyone might have against changes being carried out. In this way, the different viewpoints and evaluations are made visible; the situation becomes transparent and provides good opportunities for learning. Corrective measures are possible as a result of being explicit. Thus the individuals learn about their role in the contribution they make to the collective system of rules. The collective also learns because through the change the rules are again equated with the individual values and insights.

A second advantage of conscious learning, and therefore of explicit rules, is that rules are frequently re-established and thus acquire a collective dimension which makes them less susceptible to the effects of individuals leaving or joining the company.

At a higher level of collective learning what applies to rules is also true of insights, and at an even higher level still of principles. Argyris and Schön refer, in this connection, in their now famous book, to 'single loop' and 'double loop' learning. We distinguish between three levels of learning, which we call 'learning loops'. Collective learning can consist of *single loop* learning, *double loop* learning or *triple loop* learning.

5.3 SINGLE LOOP LEARNING

We can speak of single loop learning if collective learning brings about changes in the existing rules. Several examples of single loop learning are given below: that is *learning at the rules level*.

> An insurance company is confronted with a steadily increasing number of complaints from agents about difficulties in getting through to the office on the telephone, errors in policies, slow despatch of documents, lack of coordination between inspectors and head office and so on. A quality action is instigated, computer programs are improved, policies

are checked three times instead of twice and consultations between inspectors and head office are intensified.

A college of higher education witnesses a gradual decline in applications from new students. It is decided to intensify publicity, to produce a new prospectus, to hold open days and to mount extra-mural activities.

The work of the head of an employers' association is subjected to more and more criticism. He is sent on courses by the management, division of responsibilities between him and his staff is adjusted, and the frequency of reporting is increased, etc.

The atmosphere has sunk below zero in a personnel department; other departments have begun to complain bitterly. Two of the suspected instigators have been dismissed, other members of the staff take two two-day periods off to talk the matter through and develop new rules of behaviour.

An energy company decides to implement a series of major radical investment projects over the coming five years. The management team proposes a plan with details of the consequences of the investments for the functions and responsibilities of operators, supervisors and maintenance teams.

In one year, complaints in a small technical services company double. After an investigation, improvements are implemented in transport routes, schemes of work, telephone messages, etc.

Many of the measures applied in industry to improve quality, service and customer relations take place at the level of single loop learning. From the examples, it will probably be clear that single loop learning cannot be confused with simple, easy, conflict-free or trouble-free learning. On the contrary, even single loop learning processes may relate to radical behavioural changes.

In single loop learning, the insights (theories, assumptions, arguments) underlying the rules are scarcely, if ever, under discussion. The image of how organizations in general and your own company in particular should interrelate, and why, remains intact. No significant changes take place in the strategy, the structure, the culture or the systems of the organization. Changes in behaviour and rules are at the level of *more of the same, but better*. This level of learning poses 'how'-questions, while 'why'-questions are hardly mooted.

Single loop learning can be described as *improving*. It is

concerned with improving the rules, and solutions are sought within the existing insights and principles.

5.4 DOUBLE LOOP LEARNING

In double loop or two loop learning, not only changes in rules are called for, but also changes in the underlying insights. This phase represents *learning at the level of insight*. In the following examples of double loop learning we shall be extending the same situations described in Section 5.3.

> The insurance company begins to wonder whether perhaps different marketing strategies (such as segmentation) should be considered, and to what extent the complaints might have been caused by collective attitudes among the staff.
>
> The college begins to wonder about the curriculum it offers, and the atmosphere at the college.
>
> Members of the employers' association begin to discuss the structure of the association and the distribution of responsibilities of the office.
>
> The personnel department begins a discussion about how personnel matters could be investigated in a professional way.
>
> The management team of the energy company decides to run the project with a matrix structure, with as much involvement as possible from the processing and maintenance departments, in order to ease the transition to the new organization and give personnel the opportunity to learn on the job.
>
> When complaints in the technical service company remain at an undesirably high level, discussion of working methods is introduced into this previously very autocratically managed company.

From these examples it should be clear that here a totally different level of learning from single loop learning is concerned. Double loop learning requires a higher level of insight, the consequences are further reaching, the number of those directly or indirectly involved is higher and the learning process lasts longer. 'Why'-questions are called for; questions about the why of the rules; what they prescribe, what they permit; questions at the level of collective *knowledge* and *understanding*.

Double loop learning is typically concerned with conflicts, disputes and contradictions; not just between individuals, but also between departments, factions and other groups. That is part of it. It is precisely these signals that indicate that double loop learning is needed. To avoid debate with others at this level is to run away from the problems inextricably connected with double loop learning. The tendency to do this is, of course, understandable, since discussing insights arouses an uncertainty which many find irksome to handle. Particularly for those who have invested a great deal in the present insights there is a lot at stake, partly because they often owe their positions to them.

The most significant cause for the failure of double loop learning in problem-solving is the avoidance of mutual debate or dialogue about the background to the problems. People *run away* from the problems. One form of running away is 'doing nothing'. Problem-solving stagnates; nothing at all is solved; the organization descends into apathy and acceptance of collective incompetence. Another, less easily recognizable form of running away is escaping into action, where suggestions for problem-solving are made, but from the outset it is clear that the problem will not really be solved. Reorganization, changing the formal delineation of areas of responsibility and lines of reporting, is one of the most favoured examples of this type of escape manoeuvre. Another alternative is to *fight* and try to solve the problems politically. This is often coupled with escaping into action. Real fighting is involved when an intensive lobby is formed and heavy-handed means are employed to 'push through' a solution. For a range of different motives, the action is supported by or tolerated by different groups of individuals.

In all three of these cases, problems are solved at the wrong level, and the organization is given no opportunity to learn at the level of insight.

Double loop learning is primarily needed when external signals indicate that adjustment of the rules alone is no longer adequate: sales continue falling; the complaints keep coming in.

Secondly, double loop learning is called for when internal signals indicate that adjusting the rules might damage mutual obligations; that there are frictions concerning the rules; that people do not know collectively what they are about: in other words, when the rules are no longer understood in their mutual connection.

Both for individuals and for organizations, collective self-knowledge is primarily needed before these signals can be perceived and evaluated. There is a need for collective insight into what the organization does and does not know and understand. Insight also into what the environment thinks of it (for example the customers, suppliers, financiers). And not least insight into the connection between individual and collective behaviour and between rules and insights.

We call double loop learning *renewal*, since it relates to the renewal of insights within the existing principles.

5.5 TRIPLE LOOP LEARNING

We speak of triple loop learning when the essential principles on which the organization is founded come into discussion. When questions are raised about the position the company or section of the company wishes to adopt in the outside world, the role it aims to fulfil, the 'business it wants to be in' and the identity it has. The following examples are again related to those in Sections 5.3 and 5.4.

The insurance company begins to wonder whether it ought really to operate with agents at all, whether or not it wishes to give itself a high profile as a market leader and whether it is primarily an insurance company or an institutional investor.

Teachers in the college develop a plan to transfer, within five years, from a discipline-based to a problem-based method of education.

The employers' association calls together its members to consider in a strategic orientation round of talks the mission and goals of the association for the 1990s.

The personnel department begins discussions with the Board on whether a controlling or a supporting staff department should be developed.

The energy company, in consultation with the works council, decides not to adopt the blueprint model which would involve considerable opposition and political manipulation, but to opt for a programme of gradual development.

Two years later, the founder–director of the service company decides to step down and give his son a chance to introduce a new style of leadership into the company.

What kind of company, institution or department do we wish to be, and why? The questions which characterize triple loop learning are 'why'-questions; questions at the level of collective *will* and *being*.

Practically all organizations come up against this sort of radical process of change several times in their life span – some every five and others every fifteen years. Here, too, the key question is: when is that the case? In theory it is easy to give the answer: namely when changes at the double loop level of learning are of no assistance; when one can no longer see the point of reorganization or structural changes; and when competent key figures leave the organization.

Practical answers, however, are much more difficult to establish. At this level, too, organizations seek refuge, often to an even greater degree, in escapist or fighting behaviour. In other words, they avoid the problem. In our experience, however, it is precisely by early posing of the question of will – that is, not procrastinating – that much of the fighting and running away can be avoided. Many managers, particularly at the top, fear that through putting basic principles up for discussion the fighting and running away will only increase. Curiously enough, the existence of this fear is at the same time the reason why, if one has the courage to discuss questions of will, the fighting and running away often are greatly below expectations.

Triple loop learning can be described as *development*. It is the development of new principles, with which an organization can proceed to a subsequent phase.

5.6 ORGANIZATIONS LEARNING TO LEARN

Unfortunately there are still very many organizations which experience great difficulty in learning, or which do not move beyond the level of single loop learning. When a radical transition is necessary, they prefer to let a third party – the Advisory Commission, McKinsey or a take-over company – determine how it must be made instead of mobilizing the knowledge and ability often present in excess within their own organization. Or they continually start up new learning processes without rounding off the previous one to the level of concrete and visible behavioural change.

Organizations which begin to recognize these problems themselves, which want to examine them and draw lessons from them, are organizations which are learning to learn. They do not fall into the 'activity trap' the next time round, they do not again solve problems by dismissing their staff or by announcing yet more new structural changes.

These organizations recognize that learning at organizational level is a constantly repeated, cyclic process of doing, reflecting, thinking and deciding. Triple loop learning embraces a cycle which is measured in years. Many companies are faced with reconsideration of questions of will every seven years. Double loop learning can require as little as tens of months. Single loop learning takes place daily, weekly or monthly.

A great deal has been written in recent years about the transformation of organizations. In a relatively short time existing organizations are said to change into totally new forms. We have difficulty imagining this kind of leap for the simple reason that we have never seen such a phenomenon. We have, however, seen organizations which have learned how to learn, and have begun to approach their problems in a different way. Then they always make a leap.

5.7 IMPROVEMENT, RENEWAL AND DEVELOPMENT

The first concern of an organization is to attract competent people or to make them competent. The latter requires *individual* learning. However, an organization composed of individually competent people is not necessarily a competent organization as a result. Individually competent people can be collectively incompetent. Effective organizational behaviour, or collective competence, thus also has to be learned. All of the above-mentioned concepts of individual learning – conscious and unconscious learning, learning to learn, self-knowledge and learning phases – can apply equally well to collective learning, although the outcome may be different. This is particularly true of the concept of *learning loops*.

Collective learning thus results in different organizational behaviour or, to put it more concisely, collective learning means organizational change.

Learning loop	Learning area	Learning level	Learning result
Single	**rules**	obligation & permission	improvement
	+	+	
Double	**insights**	knowledge & understanding	renewal
	+	+	
Triple	**principles**	courage & will	development

Figure 9 Collective learning.

At the level of single loop learning this applies to changes in the *rules*; the agreements on how we collaborate and what we must do or are allowed to do. That is collective learning at the level of *ability*. This level of change leads to what we describe as *improvement*.

With double loop learning the shared *insights* forming the basis of the rules come into play: reasoning, theories, opinions and so on about the why. It is collective learning at the level of joint *knowledge* and *understanding*. To distinguish this level from the first we shall refer to it as *renewal*.

The most radical level of learning, triple loop learning, applies to changes in the communally shared *principles* on which the organization is based; what kind of organization we wish to be, the contribution we want to make, the role we choose to play and what values we consider important. It represents collective learning at the level of *courage, will* and *being*. We shall refer to this kind of change as *development*.

Part Two
Organizational Learning

Organizations do not all learn in the same way, many vary enormously. On the other hand we can distinguish a limited number of types of organization each of which shows a number of similarities in its approach towards learning. In this second part we shall describe a number of these types.

Chapter 6 focuses on what we call *entrepreneurial* organizations. Pioneering organizations especially exemplify these characteristics.

The second basic type is the *prescriptive* organization. Classical bureaucracies are mostly prescriptive organizations; Chapter 7 deals with them.

The third type, the *unlearning* organization, is described in Chapter 8. Unlearning is a dominant feature of the learning process in a bureaucracy undergoing change.

The final type that we describe is the *learning* organization. That is an organization which has the potential for *learning to learn*; Chapter 9.

The learning organizations which we know are often small organizations which either began life as such or developed from entrepreneurial organizations. It is much more interesting to examine whether and how a large prescriptive organization, a bureaucracy, can develop into a learning organization.

How such an organization will appear is a question we cannot answer for the simple reason that this sort of organization almost does not yet exist. What we can say something about is the manner in which a prescriptive organization can take its first steps in becoming a learning organization. We will undertake this in Chapter 10.

We close this part with a look at the management of collective learning processes in learning organizations. Learning processes in this sort of organization are synonymous with the processes of organizational change.

For each type of organization we describe how it learns, that is to say, develops a higher level of competence. All types, not least the learning organization, run the risk of falling to a lower level of competence, in other words, of being bogged down as an *unlearning* organization. Although this is an interesting problem, we will not be discussing it in this book.

Entrepreneurial Organizations

It is easier to become competent than to remain
competent.

6.1 WHAT IS AN ENTREPRENEURIAL ORGANIZATION?

The organizations with which we are concerned here are
generally the smaller or medium-sized, relatively young
companies. Lievegoed speaks of pioneer companies and
Mintzberg of simple structures. They are mostly companies
founded by a pioneer, who had an idea which could be made
productive. Characteristic features of this type of business are
talent or improvization, the potential for carrying out ideas and
the courage which goes with it. With youthful vitality the
product is put on the market and promoted, business functions
are developed, personnel recruited and crises overcome. New
markets are tapped and new products researched, cooperative
associations are entered into and related companies are taken
over.

The structure of this sort of company is (very) simple.
Organizational schemes hardly exist and there are relatively few
explicit rules and procedures. Tasks are allocated directly by the
founder–owner or by close associates. Power is decentralized to
a large extent. Mutual collaboration is great; coordination is
achieved largely by mutual agreement. The final criterion in
problem-solving situations is 'what would the boss think we
should do?' There are few staff departments in this sort of
company. Such as they are, they are preferably kept as small as
possible. They are seen rather as a necessary evil than as an
indispensable good.

The culture is a 'family culture' presided over by the 'father'. The dominant norm is loyalty and dedication, more so than performance and success with clients. Flexibility, mutual helpfulness, informality and devotion are key words.

Status and position are relatively unimportant except of course for the one at the top; but that position and its status are also practically unassailable. For the rest of the staff, loyalty, discipline, specialized competence and fitting in with the 'family' are what counts. Handy typifies this culture as a power culture.

The strategies of these companies are determined by 'the boss'. Strategies develop to a great extent intuitively and by trial and error. They have a relatively short time-span and are mostly focus strategies.

The boss or bosses at the top are more leaders than managers. Their leadership is based on power plus either charisma and/or professional expertise. Their style of leadership is dominated by two extremes: on the one hand 'telling', that is to say, stating without much explanation what is required and how; on the other hand complete delegation, which is naturally only used with employees who enjoy complete confidence.

These companies do particularly well in a rapidly expanding, often not too easy, but not unfriendly market.

6.2 FEATURES OF THE LEARNING PROCESS

Such organizations learn a great deal and, in the growth phases, often very quickly. The way in which they learn has a number of interconnected features which largely correspond to how young people learn. We can summarize them with the term *entrepreneurialism*. Just like the type of organizations and the environment in which they operate, the learning process is almost completely an *entrepreneurial process*. At every turn new things are learned: in the first phase, learning production, promotion, selling and administration; in the next phase, learning development of new products and new markets; then, learning to develop cooperative links with other organizations. And, as a side effect, learning how to overcome conflicts, crises, and so on.

These organizations learn principally through *doing*, experimentation and experience. The overwhelming majority of employees of this sort of company are doers; there are few

Strategy	**Aggressive strategy** • short-term • (pro)active • focus/niche • intuitive
Structure	**Simple** • centralisation • only top management and operational • informal
Culture	**Power culture** • loyalty • large family • devotion, mutual helpfulness • informality • discipline
Systems	**Necessary evil**

Table 1 Distinctive features of an 'entrepreneurial organization'.

thinkers and reflecters and they are not popular. *Ability* and *courage* are characteristics of these organizations.

The most important criterion in developing new strategies or approaching new activities is always: shall we succeed, can we do it? Little attention is paid to collective analysis or theorizing. The company either does not have or will not make time for that sort of thing. The same applies even more so to reflecting and thinking. There is a strong motivation towards action. Insofar as anything is done about acquisition of new knowledge or insight, it is directed exclusively towards being able to do something with it. The few educational courses followed are courses where the company has direct profit from them. Where we postulated that organizations of this sort learn by doing, this is particularly true for employees who belong to the operational core. A characteristic feature is in particular not only a lack of respect for analysis, theorizing and reflection but also a marked division between deciding and doing. In this sort of organization what applies is simply that the top decides and the operational departments execute.

When this picture is compared with the learning cycle, the conclusion is clearly that these organizations learn using only *one* track; they learn 'one-sidedly'.

Figure 10 The entrepreneurial organization.

Another salient feature is that entrepreneurial organizations learn *unconsciously*, to a great extent; via the mechanisms of *imitation* on the one hand and *reward* and *punishment* on the other. Imitation is the dominant mechanism for learning internal organizational behaviour through picking up the art (from 'the boss' and his associates, the elite). Anyone wishing to know how this sort of company functions internally would have to do little more than get to know 'the boss'. The rules for cooperation are therefore largely implicit. They are not based on mutual agreements but on loyalty to the top.

External organizational behaviour is learned via the mechanisms of reward and punishment, especially reward and punishment from the outside, that is to say, the markets, customers and other interested parties. Behaviour which is rewarded by the outside is quickly adopted by everyone. Behaviour which is not valued externally is quickly dropped. In fact, the only criterion for outside behaviour that really counts is success.

In these organizations collective learning takes place almost exclusively at the *single loop* level, the level of *improvement*. There is little room for double loop learning, learning at the level of insights, and when it does occur it is extremely laborious. Triple loop learning, learning at the level of principles is taboo in this type of organization, or to put it better, it is reserved exclusively for the top. When these organizations are operating successfully, it can be observed that in the course of years rules and insights are raised to the level of principles ('that's just the way we do things here') and, as a result, cannot be discussed. This has the effect that, because of the success of the organization, collective learning recedes even further. The organization slowly changes from a construction to a system.

Summary: entrepreneurial organizations learn one-sidedly; their learning is directed towards ability and action; it is largely unconscious and almost exclusively at the level of improvement.

6.3 THE WEAKNESS OF ENTREPRENEURIAL ORGANIZATIONS

Entrepreneurial organizations can continue successfully in this way for years if not for decades. The consequences of this learning process are mostly only visible when an incisive discontinuity arises.

The first discontinuity occurs when radical changes take place outside, especially in the market. Members of the organization suddenly find themselves having to determine what they must do and what they are allowed to do. These questions have previously received little attention. Even worse, the rules about operating in the market and the environment are largely implicit and have been learned unconsciously, focusing on ability. Now, even insights have to be discussed, which requires skills the company has scarcely developed and about which knowledge is lacking. In contrast with bureaucracies, these organizations have few 'reservoirs of knowledge' in the form of staff and the like. The usual reaction is to increase their efforts; a strategy of 'more of the same'. A reaction which at best amounts to a stay of execution.

Another discontinuity which is perhaps even more incisive, occurs when 'the boss' relinquishes control. In this case, the symbol of corporate identity is no longer present, and the organization is faced with the question: what kind of company do we wish to be? It is a question about which members of the company have till then never had to think and have never been allowed to think. The result is that the organization becomes powerless and directionless. The usual reaction to such a crisis is to try to appoint another 'strong man' of the same kind as quickly as possible. This approach is often destined to fail, and even when it succeeds, it merely delays the crisis until the demise of the new boss.

6.4 FROM AN ENTREPRENEURIAL ORGANIZATION TO A LEARNING ORGANIZATION

If normal behaviour does not seem to be working, this sort of organization unfortunately often takes steps which turn it into the second type: a bureaucracy, or prescriptive organization, instead of a learning organization. The standard scenario is nearly always to bring in 'management' from the outside: a new type of director, supported by managers and management experts, who then resolutely set about what is called the installation of structure; the creation of hierarchical levels; the founding of staff departments; the setting up of function, task and responsibility descriptions; the introduction of procedures and regulations; the development of systems.

In short, they do precisely what is presented in the literature on developmental phases as natural, necessary and inevitable. They organize, and this almost always has the same outcome: bureaucratization.

In itself, this reaction seems logical. By recruiting experts from outside, the gap in knowledge and insight is filled, and by imposing structure, order is brought into what is expected of everyone in the organization: what people are allowed to do and what they must do. The mistake is in the *manner* of doing this.

Attempts to eliminate the existing one-sidedness in learning potential by learning together are hardly ever encountered. In other words, an attempt to turn it into a learning organization is seldom undertaken. As a result, within the space of a few years, a previously vital organization can often degenerate into a passive, reactive company with a high turnover of personnel, especially if the branch of the industry is attractive.

There is a second obstacle to the approach we have described, if an entrepreneurial organization is to become a learning organization. It will then be necessary to choose an approach in which one begins with the greatest omission in the learning potential of the organization. This is usually learning to solve collectively the question: what sort of company do we actually want to be? Thus *triple loop learning* arises. Particularly when the crisis has been caused by the boss leaving, the above is the most important question. And particularly in times of crisis this question is not asked. On the contrary, possibilities for action are sought. Changing into a learning organization requires an answer to the identity question. Only when this question has been answered will it be possible to answer questions such as: what must we do? What are we allowed to do? Which insights do we share?

If they succeed in collectively finding an answer to the identity question, entrepreneurial organizations do not necessarily have to transform into prescriptive systems. They can still make the leap towards becoming learning organizations. We are fortunate in knowing companies which have actually accomplished this leap.

Prescriptive Organizations

Bureaucracy rewards you for not doing wrong,
rather than for actually doing well.

7.1 WHAT IS A PRESCRIPTIVE ORGANIZATION?

The type of organization we are concerned with here is the classical bureaucracy, described by Mintzberg as *machine bureaucracy*. The word 'machine' is intended here as a metaphor to characterize this type of organization: men and materials act as small cogs in a mechanical whole. Such organizations are mostly large and old, concentrating on the mass production of a standardized range of products and services. Good examples are steelworks, car factories, railway companies, telephone companies, banks, insurance companies and government-run firms. We owe our welfare largely to this type of organization. By standardizing production processes as extensively as possible they manage to keep costs and prices to a minimum while continuously producing the maximum amount of products and services.

Organization in this type of company has been so often described in so many books that we will content ourselves here with a summary of the main features of the structure, culture, systems and strategy. In Table 2, an extensive summing up is given using key words.

The structure is the classical, centralist, hierarchical, functional, line–staff structure, with extensive specialist division of responsibilities. The culture is a role culture (position, status) in which rationality, logic, justice and efficiency are the key values. The strategy is directed towards continuity and control of the environment. Management systems are directed towards the creation of order and control of deviations from the desired

Strategy	**Command strategy**
	• long term
	• reactive, defensive
	• costs/market leadership
	• (pre)caution
Structure	**Classical functional line-staff structure**
	• functional organizational structure, powers, responsibilities
	• separate staff and line organization
	• far reaching specialization
	• many hierarchical levels
	• centralization: formal power with strategic top
	• many formal rules, procedures, systems
Culture	**Role culture**
	• rationality and logic
	• efficiency, doing a good job
	• stability, reduction of insecurity
	• formalistic and mechanistic
	• rules are rules
	• sensitive to status and position
	• avoidance of conflict
Systems	**Control**
	• order
	• measurement and rules
	• analytical
	• uniform
	• reactive

Table 2 The distinctive features of a 'prescriptive organization'.

norms. Systems are mostly reactive with the accent on establishing developments which can subsequently lead to greater insight by means of analyses.

A bureaucracy is an organization in which a relatively large amount of education is carried out, and a great deal is learned, even if it is one-sided, by individuals. At the same time it is an organization which collectively experiences great difficulties in learning, more so than any other type of organization.

7.2 THESE ORGANIZATIONS HAVE LEARNING DIFFICULTIES

Organizations learn by collectively examining problems, investigating the causes, thinking out and testing new approaches, and then the cycle can begin again.

However, the organizations of bureaucracies, with conscious or unconscious intent, are directed, sometimes down to the smallest details, at preventing problems, and thus also preventing *learning*. This is the common thread which runs through and connects the strategy, culture, structure and systems of these organizations. The essential organizational features have a reinforcing effect on each other and processes that make these organizations lack the *need*, the *courage*, the *will* and the *ability* to learn.

They do not need to learn

External strategies are aimed at controlling the environment and keeping it stable. Assuming that this succeeds, a structure is developed internally in which departments are grouped according to function, and tasks are divided up as extensively as possible into individually specialized activities.

In such a structure the necessity for task-oriented cooperation is reduced to a minimum and therefore so is the need for learning through interpersonal interaction. Any cooperation which does occur is mainly restricted to a particular functional department, that is, between like-minded and similarly attuned individuals. If problems do arise, the solution is either to iron them out – one of the most important roles of middle management – or to state even more precisely where one person's responsibility ends and another's begins.

Problems are either 'solved' by fine-tuning the procedures or passed upwards to the next level. These managers often operate according to the principle 'a problem shared is a problem halved'.

They lack the courage to learn

One of the basic principles – values if you like – underlying this sort of organization is that organizational action must be rational and logical. These values naturally have their good side, and can easily be explained from the history of the origin of these prescriptive organizations. However, they also undermine many people's courage to learn. Human behaviour is not controlled exclusively by reason but also by emotion and is therefore not simply rational and logical, although it is almost a heresy to admit this.

In our opinion, this is one of the most significant causes for the discrepancy so often encountered in these organizations between what is said and what is done. Argyris and Schön speak of a difference between 'espoused theory' and 'theory in use'. This can be expressed in terms of a *talk theory* and an *action theory*. By a 'talk theory' we mean the theories and concepts by which people *say* their actions are determined. The term 'action theory' refers to concepts and theories which *explain* ultimate actions.

Regarding their style of leadership managers can claim that their actions are participative and fed by efforts to let the employees reach their optimum potential. Observation of their behaviour, however, gives the impression that they are really aiming to dominate their staff and manipulate them by rehearsed dictates. There may be indications that the managers say they are open to other people's ideas but then structure meetings so that there is no time for discussion and subsequently outside meetings they avoid contact by always being absent.

In no other organization is there so great a discrepancy between what is said and what is done as in a prescriptive organization. The emphasis is not so much on tackling problems collectively, but more on talking about them collectively. People – managers, employees, members of staff – try to convince each other, and presumably also themselves, via reports and presentations full of rhetoric and rationalizations, that they know what must be done and how they must do it.

Prescriptive organizations are 'persuasion organizations'. Talking about 'theory in use', about what is actually done, is avoided as much as possible for fear of being accused of illogicality or irrationality. If things turn out well, there is a large number of defensive mechanisms ready which have individual powerlessness as a common denominator. If things go wrong, the favourite game is to lay the blame on someone else. Sometimes that means 'them': the other department, the management, the staff, and if that is too definite, there is always 'the system'.

In an organization where emotions, uncertainty and conflicts are to be avoided, defensiveness can lead to a situation where not much criticism is expressed. The safest reaction is to withdraw to your own domain and responsibilities because your flank is unguarded. In this way criticism can be evaded.

However, the price is that without criticism there can be no learning.

They lack the will to learn

Being prepared to take risks is an essential prerequisite for learning. Situations in which learning is necessary contain risks by definition, because the new circumstances are unknown and could present surprises. Initiative and testing new ideas predictably lead to errors; you learn from doing and the mistakes are experiences which can increase the effectiveness of learning. In bureaucracies, however, mistakes are often better remembered than successful initiatives. Mistakes are used as a means of fine-tuning the rules to gain better control; they are used as a means of finding a 'scapegoat' to underline the value of the rules and procedures. This makes avoiding mistakes a much more sensible way of obtaining a good appraisal report than showing initiative. Appraisal systems sometimes show mistakes in absolute terms rather than as a percentage of innovative activity. Passivity and thus freedom from error show up better than a spirit of enterprise with the inevitable failures. This results in the lack of the will to learn; you are rewarded for not doing wrong rather than for doing well.

They lack the ability to learn

This is the logical sequel to the above. An organization in which little is learned is slow to develop the ability to learn.

We already said that in entrepreneurial organizations learning is mainly through doing. Bureaucracies are much less one-sided, but in these organizations thinking, doing and deciding are clearly distinguished from each other. *Managerial staff*, especially staff advisers, *do the thinking*. Operational units act on their ideas. *Decisions* are made by the line, especially the top management. The problem is combining thinking, deciding and doing. This is not confined to organizational distinctions, and we can trace the distinctions back to learning styles: 'thinkers' predominate at staff departmental level; 'doers' in the operational units and 'deciders' are found at the top.

Readers who themselves work in a bureaucracy will perhaps accuse us of having sketched a caricature. Disregarding any possible exaggeration, the problem remains that bureaucracies

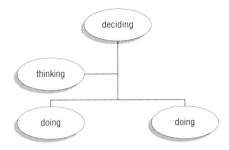

Figure 11 Division of thinking, doing and deciding.

have great difficulties with learning because the organization invokes a number of mutually supporting processes in order not to need, to dare or to be willing to learn.

Bureaucracies are in a vicious circle. Learning potential is low and will remain low as long as there is no pressure from outside to change. If, however, that is the case, the potential is then lacking and the organization will try to remove the pressure and so it goes on. Bureaucracies which must change or want to change are faced with the same task as Baron von Münchhausen, who found himself in the morass on his horse. Is it possible to pull yourself out by your own hair?

7.3 THE ROLE OF EDUCATION

Prescriptive organizations, especially the larger companies, undertake a great deal of educational training. The training activities mostly take place in two, and in the larger ones three, functional staff departments, namely: the education department, the training department and the management development department.

The education department is responsible for the education (in the narrower sense) of employees. It is here for the most part a matter of specialist education. Its main responsibility is selecting and guiding employees towards existing professional education courses, which have often been developed at the level of a particular branch of industry and therefore in consultation with similar companies. Sometimes, however, the required specialist skills are so specific that the company has developed a programme which is completely its own, with or without the help of an educational institution, and intended exclusively for the company's own employees.

Besides this, many companies have a training department which provides or arranges for training in specific skills such as chairing a meeting, presentation, interviewing and coaching.

It is typical that these companies often have a separate department for providing management education (let it be said, for employees above a certain level or salary scale). These courses, and this must be quite clear, confine themselves to functional aspects of management: financial management and personnel management, possibly combined within a business administration course.

Nearly all the courses mentioned, even if they are exclusively designed for the company's own employees, are individual courses, directed towards the development of the individual skills required in the various functions. There is relatively little provision for collective education, that is, conscious improvement of the learning potential of the organization as a whole. The many tentative steps which have been taken in this direction have so far not been very successful.

This is easy to explain. So long as the traditional activities intended for individual learning continue uncurtailed, collective learning targets will have little chance of success. That is to say, this is an attempt to combine two mutually contradictory methods of learning. Collective education can only succeed when individual education is made subordinate to it. In other words it can do no more than fulfil a supplementary function. By making a split between education and training, separating hierarchical levels and placing the emphasis on specialist education and functional management education, all the previously mentioned mechanisms and processes are once again intensified: thinking in terms of functional competences and responsibilities, rationalization, persuading and defending; the 'them'-syndrome and the distinction between thinking, doing and deciding.

Meanwhile a remarkable situation exists in that the minds of employees of prescriptive organizations are storing a great deal of (especially) knowledge and insights – often far more than is needed for their function. At the same time that organization is powerless to mobilize this knowledge and put it to useful effect. That is how it can be explained that organizational consulting companies earn a fat living from precisely this sort of company; they give back the knowledge they have gained from the organization in a handsome report which thereby reinforces its lack of learning potential.

If the consultant's advice is followed and is unsuccessful, then the consultant becomes the 'scapegoat', and the organization's belief in its own insights and principles is further reinforced.

7.4 A PRESCRIPTIVE LEARNING SYSTEM

As we said in Section 2.5, we are concerned with a system when the social construction begins to lead such a life of its own and show its own legalities that the individual members come to believe they have little influence over it. More than for any other type of system this applies to a bureaucracy. It is largely a system of such mutually cooperative and intensifying processes that the members scarcely feel capable of behaving otherwise than as an element of that system.

Members also perceive it as a system, as anyone would agree who has taken part in a few 'back-home' sessions at the end of a traditional educational course. At 'come-back days' or 'after-burners', or whatever jargon may be devised for it, it turns out that practically nobody has felt that they could do anything more with what they have learned than become a little more competent themselves.

This is how the self-fulfilling prophesy arises and it becomes a vicious circle; the more your own organization is perceived as a system, a whole made up of little cogs, the more you begin to behave according to the system, like a little cog-wheel. The wheel continues to turn *within* the machine regardless of what the wheel has learned on a course *outside* the machine.

In such an organization all sorts of mechanisms obstruct learning. Even single loop learning often occurs with the greatest difficulty. Committees or work groups, the most widely tried form of organizational learning, often spend years developing or adapting regulations 'relating to' or 'concerning' for example: car allowances, induction, processing of mail, performance reviews, using public relations services, signing authorities, legal and judicial affairs, demarcation between staff in the office and in the field, and frequency of spot checks on truck drivers. The main problem all these committees encounter is having their findings implemented in the organization. Often the representatives in these committees have no mandate to make agreements, with the result that the deliberations are suspended or limited to thinking and are not rounded off with deciding and doing. The learning cycle is not completed.

The same applies even more so with double loop learning. The favourite method here is also the committee: for example the restructuring committee or committee for preparation of information planning and so forth. In bureaucracies a great deal of double loop learning takes place in committees but it is again one-sided, on the level of talk theories. The learning cycle is not completed because decisions are not made or not carried out. As a result, the organization has failed to learn.

Sometimes the need for change is so urgent that the bureaucracy develops a project organization, which is totally separate from the existing organization. The task of the manager of this unit is principally to protect this activity from the logic of the bureaucracy.

Prescriptive organizations are successful at fitting new members into the company and teaching them individually how to behave. This is partly a conscious process but mostly unconscious. Not all teachers realize it, but one of the main functions of training courses is to condition employees and fit their skills to the demands of the system. This can be seen from the style of the courses; they are typically 'persuasive courses'. Courses are therefore also an important coordination mechanism.

Even leadership style is, often unconsciously, directed towards this goal. The overwhelming majority of managers score highest in the Hersey and Blanchard model on 'selling' style: selling, persuading. This leadership implicitly presupposes a relatively low level of task-maturity among subordinates, an assumption which permeates all levels of the hierarchy. In terms of transactional analysis: it is an organization in which cooperation is dominated on the psychological level by parent–child transactions between the hierarchical levels. In communication it is true that opinions are exchanged which sound adult enough. However, in the manner in which they approach each other the inequality is always quite subtly emphasized. Everyone feels that they are being lectured and that they ought to behave as if they are convinced. Those who do not let themselves be convinced immediately will learn soon enough from the supplementary and often refined mechanisms of reward and punishment: performance appraisal interviews or promotion and reward systems.

Sociologists call this type of system a *reification*: an organization which is seen by its members as an entity, the continuation of which is completely independent from its members and in which all aspects and elements are interconnected. It is also an organization which creates processes which have a compulsive character for its members. Setting out from this interpretation, problems are considered as caused by and inherent in the organization. The problems thus must also be solved by this organization which is, however, something which the organization cannot do. And so one is caught in one's own net.

Unlearning Organizations

If it hurts, it works.

8.1 WHAT IS AN UNLEARNING ORGANIZATION?

This chapter is again about bureaucracies, therefore prescriptive organizations, but about bureaucracies undergoing change. Bureaucracies change with extreme difficulty. At the same time a very large proportion of this sort of organization is constantly occupied in bringing about organizational changes. Some companies seem almost addicted to it. And nearly always it is a question of changes in the structure of the organization, in other words, reorganization.

In the 1980s the insight slowly began to emerge that structural changes alone are often not very effective. The words of the song may change but the tune remains the same. People began to realize that structural changes must be accompanied by cultural changes, and also that change is a learning process. Thanks to these insights, demand for 'tailor-made, in-company educational courses' has arisen in precisely these organizations.

Nevertheless in prescriptive organizations the so-called 'design' or 'blueprint' method is still the preferred form of organizational change. It is a method which leads to the learning processes becoming prescriptive, with its most dominant feature being that one must *unlearn*. Hence the fact that we give these prescriptive organizations undergoing change the name 'unlearning organizations'.

8.2 REORGANIZATION PROCESSES VERSUS THOSE OF BEHAVIOURAL CHANGE

The *design* or *blueprint* method can roughly be described as follows: a committee of line managers and staff members, whether or not supported by consultants, first makes as good and complete a blueprint as possible of the future desired organization – in terms of strategy, structure, systems and culture – and then tries in every way to convince the employees concerned of the correctness of that blueprint; a process of persuasion which is nearly always in the first instance accompanied to a greater or lesser degree by *resistance*.

The essential hallmark of this blueprint model is that the whole process of organizational change is split into two processes: a thought process, in which, at the level of talk theory, agreement is sought about the new strategy, structure, culture and systems; and an implementation process, when these talk theories have to be converted into action theories. The first process we call the process of *reorganization* and the second, the process of *behavioural change*. In unlearning organizations these are separate processes.

The implicit view, still held by very many managers who use this approach, is that a process of change is complete when the process of reorganization is complete. This has the effect that little attention is paid to the subsequent process of behavioural change, with the obvious assumption that the reorganization will automatically lead to different behaviour. In fact, the opposite is true; it is precisely the process of behavioural change that costs the most time, trouble and energy. This is a radical learning process for which luckily in recent years there has been an increase in understanding. It is a learning process that is principally an unlearning process.

8.3 FEATURES OF THE LEARNING PROCESS

In this process it is a matter of learning together to behave in agreement with the new rules, insights or even principles which originate from the blueprint.

We have in past years been so much under the impression that there is such a degree of difficulty, complexity and often painfulness associated with this sort of learning process that we are more surprised when organizational changes of this type are successful, and therefore are converted into a change in behaviour, than when they are partly or wholly unsuccessful.

Quite differently from what people in these organizations are accustomed to, this learning process is a *collective* process: learning with each other, old hands together with newcomers, but also higher echelons with the more lowly. A learning process both for those who have 'thought it out' and for those who must 'carry it out'; each and all learning at the same time.

However, this is also an *imposed* learning process. Everybody to whom the reorganization is applicable has to take part regardless of the question of whether they contributed to planning the new organization. Naturally there is everything to be said for letting those concerned participate as far as possible in the planning of the blueprint for the future. However, whether one has participated or not, and whether one was in agreement or not, everyone will have to fit in with it.

A third unusual feature for prescriptive organizations is that this is a learning process *without teachers*. Those who contributed to the blueprint have a cognitive advantage, but this does not necessarily mean that they will be any better than others at 'playing' the new organization. The fact of having contributed to a decision about, for example, a structure in which more delegation occurs, does not mean that you can therefore do it any better. In short, everyone is equally competent, or, to put it better, equally incompetent. Since everyone has grown up in the old organization with its work practices and methods, everyone is in the same situation, regardless of role, status and position.

'Bosses' are not necessarily more competent than subordinates. That is a new and even a cultural breakthrough. One can generalize by saying that new, young employees – uncontaminated as they are by the old ideas – are often the fastest at being able to pick up the new behaviour. The most dominant feature, however, is that the learning process is primarily a process of *unlearning*. It is not just a question of learning new behaviour and learning new knowledge and insights. The real difficulty is in unlearning old behaviour. Certainly, this is the case if this old behaviour was, to a large extent, learned unconsciously by imitation, reward and punishment. Old emotions come to the surface again: behaviour which used to be rewarded is now punished. Conversely, people are now respected for behaviour which was not previously permitted. Suddenly, it is no longer any good being punctual or avoiding conflicts and 'covering the boss' no longer works. Suddenly, your degree has become of less value, you have to monitor your own budget, to delegate downwards and to say what you think. If ever it was the case that learning is a painful process, 'if it hurts, it works', it applies first of all to unlearning. What is also very painful is the dishonesty and humiliation. Newcomers overtake old timers by exhibiting behaviour which used to be an obstacle to promotion. But you have to join in because of the background threats of demotion, transfer, or perhaps even being phased out or dismissed.

8.4 THE ROLE OF EDUCATION

It is fairly obvious how important it is to support learning processes of this sort with (collective) educational courses. Classical educational courses are those in which learning goals are derived from the skill requirements set by the new organization, in which, consequently, learning requirements are listed, learning strategy and prescriptive methods are developed and finally an often highly structured programme is worked out for each target group. These courses are aimed at the successive acquisition of the required knowledge and insight, the required skills and attitudes. Often prescriptive courses mean education by persuasion. This continues until a level of competence is reached at which the learning process can be taken over and continued using the old methods of leadership, imitation, reward and punishment.

Even though here it is a matter of classical education, there is nevertheless an essential difference from comparable courses for individuals. During the education the participants exchange notes on what they are thinking and experiencing. If the level of acceptance for the new organization is low, then the course is one of the most important forums for expressing dissatisfaction or making new proposals. That can be very awkward for course leaders; groups are much more difficult to persuade than individuals or newcomers. ('If you teach a group of people to do the washing up, you should not be surprised if they challenge the layout of the kitchen.')

At the same time this offers the possibility of channelling dissatisfaction or new ideas into positive contributions to the reorganization process via educational courses. However, that requires more than traditional competence from course tutors. In addition they will then need to have a position in the organization so as to be *able* to join in doing something as well as a contract with the instigator of the reorganization so as to be *permitted* to join in doing something.

8.5 RELATIONS AND FRICTION BETWEEN PROCESSES OF REORGANIZING AND BEHAVIOURAL CHANGE

Although the processes of reorganization and behavioural change are separate processes, they influence and stimulate each other. Thus in the initial stages the process of reorganization provides the stimulus for the process of behavioural change. In later stages, however, they hinder each other.

One of the most awkward problems in this sort of organizational change is that reorganization processes take a different course and have different dynamics from behavioural change processes. Processes of organizational change, however whimsical they may be in practice, are essentially processes of *linear succession*, through which, in the course of time, one organizational aspect is brought close to another. Everything cannot be changed in one process at the same time. One must choose; if we begin with structure, is the process to start at the top, or lower down at departmental level? Or, do we first tackle culture? And if so, at what do we then aim first? Customer orientation, style of leadership or ways of dealing with conflict? Or, is it better to start with a change of strategy? The choice depends for example on where most of the energy is to be found, or where the need is most urgent. Practice shows an extremely capricious course of constantly changing combinations of choices.

Processes of behavioural change by contrast are *cyclic*, self-supporting processes, from which, given time, a steady increase in the level of competence can be expected. This is true of individual learning but even more so of a collective learning process.

These two processes are mutually disruptive, because of their essentially divergent dynamics. The process of reorganization, which begins as the motor behind the process of behavioural change, eventually starts to have a braking effect on this same process. A number of examples illustrate what a frustrating effect this can have.

Within the framework of a recently decentralized structure, the divisional director undertakes to defend assertively his budget for the year; six months later a minus sign appears on his confidential appraisal report under the heading: working with others.

Stimulated to more proactive behaviour, an administrator submits on his own initiative a summary of financial opportunities and threats that he has become aware of; it stays in his head of department's drawer on the grounds of lack of accuracy and incompleteness, and it is made clear to him that this is the task of marketing.

Within the framework of a move to provide an improved service, sales representatives decide to make more regular visits to customers; six months later their bonus is cut for having overstepped the permitted mileage limits.

Acting entirely within the increased room to manoeuvre conferred upon her, a marketing manager concludes a contract with a client; a week later, it appears that the price control department has induced the marketing director to declare the contract invalid. A week after this the marketing manager is given a lecture by a member of the Board who asks why she did not sort out the problem herself with the client; doesn't she realize that her room for manoeuvre has been increased? In passing the member of the Board of Management informs her that he himself has sorted it out quickly.

'We must become more open'. At last the works manager summons up the courage to say what he thinks at the meeting. Then the chairman explains that due to modifications to internal management structure it has been decided that this kind of contribution no longer comes under works consultation, but belongs to policy discussions. In the lunch break the works manager is asked sympathetically if there is any trouble at home.

From now on, unit management requires supporting departments to send the operational units a note specifying services rendered by them. Six months later, at a management meeting the director expresses her concern that there is too much negotiating and not enough cooperation.

These frictions are the result of the fact that the two processes do not go forward in parallel with each other. There is, considering the different progress of them, very little that can be done about it. It does not matter whether you begin with structure or with culture, whether bottom-up or top-down approaches are adopted, whether you proceed department by department or aspect by aspect; the symptoms will still continue to appear. The two processes must of course be carefully matched with each other, but if you do this with the aim of preventing this kind of phenomenon, you will always end up being disappointed. The friction symptoms we have mentioned are inevitable. They should be regarded as an *opportunity* rather than a threat.

8.6 FROM A PRESCRIPTIVE TO A LEARNING ORGANIZATION

In the initial phase of the organizational change the process of reorganization gives impetus to the process of behavioural change. Friction occurs somewhat later.

By then, the process of behavioural change has entered a phase where skills newly learned collectively begin to clash with the organization; with existing rules, insights and possibly even principles. Talk theories have been collectively transformed into action theories, and again the inaccuracies or incompletenesses in the talk theories arise.

This may be seen as a threat, but may also be an opportunity. For this is just the moment to turn the tables and let the process of behavioural change become the motor behind the process of reorganization. That is the moment to change from a prescriptive organization to a learning one.

Learning Organizations

> Organizations under great pressure seldom
> change their opinion. The same is true of
> organizations which have nothing to do.
>
> *Freely after Nietzsche*

9.1 WHAT IS A LEARNING ORGANIZATION?

Essentially, learning organizations are not only capable of learning, but also of *learning to learn*. In other words, they are not only able to *become* competent but also to *remain* competent.

There are many entrepreneurial and also prescriptive organizations which have been successful in reaching an extremely high level of competence. This is true of nearly all the bureaucracies with high scores in *In Search of Excellence* or in *Fortune's* list. However, competence is linked to time and situation. If the situation changes, the criteria for competence also change, so it is possible that organizations which were once competent can very quickly become incompetent.

Learning organizations have mastered the art of adapting quickly on the one hand and preserving their own direction and identity on the other. This is what we understand by development. Development means adaptation without losing identity; reaction as well as proaction; letting yourself be influenced by the environment as well as exercising influence on the environment.

Development is the key concept for the learning organization. It requires the potential to learn collectively at the highest and also the most difficult level of all: triple loop learning, at the level of principles.

9.2 WHAT DO LEARNING ORGANIZATIONS LOOK LIKE?

In the following sections we describe the learning principles which an organization must fulfil if it wishes to be called a learning organization. Tested by these principles we know of relatively few organizations which meet with our definition, and certainly no large post-bureaucratic organizations.

The learning organizations we do know are small, mostly still young organizations which either started as such or grew out of entrepreneurial organizations. They are nearly always companies with complex and constantly changing working processes which require a high degree of training and professionalism.

In terms of their features, these organizations come closest to what Mintzberg calls the 'adhocracy' (see Table 3).

The learning organization is currently of great interest to scientists, consultants and managers alike. Many see this organization as the desired form for bureaucracies which are bogged down. However, the adhocracy is too simple to function as a model here. The scale, extent, complexity and interdependencies of the working processes in bureaucracies are too great for it. An adhocracy can hardly be expected to produce cars.

For this sort of working process we do not know the answer to the question: what might a learning organization look like? The reason for this is that we do not know of any bureaucracy which has been able to make the transition to a learning organization completely successfully. The question is not really relevant. Asking the question reflects a way of thinking about change which is characteristic of the prescriptive organization. A learning organization does not ask that question, but develops its own forms while learning. A more important question is: how can you make an organization which has expanded naturally into a prescriptive organization make the leap towards a learning organization? We shall deal with this question in the next chapter.

So we do not know precisely what learning organizations (must) precisely look like. But, what we do have the courage to say is something about the learning principles which underlie a learning organization; principles which must make meta-learning possible, thus preventing learning organizations from making the same mistakes as entrepreneurial and prescriptive organizations.

Strategy	**Continued development**
	• mission directed
	• short and medium term
	• rational and intuitive
	• active and proactive
	• various focuses
Structure	**Organic networks**
	• loosely combined units and teams based around product and market combinations
	• decentralization
	• mixing of thinkers (staff) and doers (line)
	• coordination through discussion
Culture	**Task-oriented culture**
	• flexible
	• problem oriented
	• creative
Systems	**Supportive**
	• information for reflection, 'on the system'
	• information for action, 'in the system'
	• dealing with complexity

Table 3 The distinctive features of the 'learning organization'.

9.3 PROBLEM-ORIENTED, CYCLIC LEARNING AND LEARNING BY DOING

The learning processes in a learning organization are *problem oriented*. They are initiated and controlled by existing or anticipated problems. Learning therefore takes place whenever the present situation does not match the desired situation. Indeed, that is the definition of a problem. In this respect especially the learning organization diverges from the prescriptive organization which is designed to prevent the occurrence of problems as far as possible. By contrast, in a learning organization problems are seen as interesting indicators of changes that might be needed; of necessary learning processes.

Problems determine not only what must be learned and how, but also *who* must be concerned in the learning process: those are the people who because of their involvement or competence are connected with the problem or the solution of it.

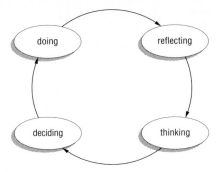

Figure 12 The learning organization.

Problem-oriented learning implies at the same time that learning is related to work. Learning takes place *on the job*. The learning processes are linked to the work processes. A workplace is also a learning situation and a task is likewise an exercise. Finally problem-oriented learning is also cyclic learning: doing → reflecting → thinking → deciding. In a learning organization, *thinking* and *doing* are not separate, but are linked together via *reflecting* and *deciding* (see Figure 12).

9.4 COLLECTIVE LEARNING

The learning organization diverges from both entrepreneurial and prescriptive organizations because in the learning organization learning is to a great extent *collective*. Of course, individual learning processes do take place. However, the emphasis is on learning together in teams. And not just within a division, department or group, and not only at one level, but also between departments, divisions, groups and between the different levels.

Team learning is such a dominant feature of the learning organization that many writers implicitly or explicitly advocate building up the organization around these learning teams, instead of following the classical model based on line and staff departments.

Bomers, for example, maintains that *multidimensional* teams represent the building blocks of learning organizations.

These are teams which are so composed that a mix of knowledge, insights and skills, as well as characters, values, roles and functions are represented. Does this mean that teams will replace staff and line departments in learning organizations, and that hierarchical echelons will disappear? We think not. Many working processes are so specialized and complex that vertical and horizontal separations are inevitable. Boundaries will thus always reappear, but the choice of boundaries can always be discussed. That is also one of the most important reasons for the continual reorganizations in prescriptive organizations. But that often solves very little as there is no best way of 'cutting'. The challenge for the learning organization is precisely to continue to 'paste over' all these boundaries that have thus arisen, by means of collective learning – in teams, working parties and task forces.

The main cause for poor collective learning potential in prescriptive organizations is not the existence of echelons or functional line and staff departments, but poor mutual cooperation or even the avoidance of it between echelons and departments. Learning in prescriptive organizations is directed towards the actual function of the individual or the department as a cog in the whole machine instead of focusing on the interdependencies between these cogs. In prescriptive organizations boundaries thereby quickly result in separations offering the individual or the department the security needed to develop an identity of its own apart from the rest: 'them' or the others. Instead of the boundary being a means of making contact and giving form to communication between components, the boundary becomes a barrier to contact. 'No-man's-lands' grow up between departments, as a result of which the question of the solution of a problem quickly develops into a discussion of the optimum demarcation of authorities and accountabilities.

In a learning organization, which has the realization of the work as its orientation, the boundary is a pragmatic, often temporary choice intended as a means of facilitating cooperation. The boundary provides clarity about each other's position and identity. In a learning organization the boundaries are places where intensive contact is needed, because it is precisely there that an exchange of ideas takes place between the separate sections and cooperation is thus crucial.

Departments are interlinked and made mutually inter-dependent through the work process. In a learning organization, changes occur at the points of contact in the organization where, from the meeting of the different angles of incidence, interests and contributions, *learning* takes place.

9.5 CONSCIOUS LEARNING

A learning organization stimulates *conscious* learning. This serves to make learning both complementary and constructive (see Chapter 3).

Conscious learning is *methodical* learning with the most important method being mutual questioning. Conscious learning requires collective will, courage and knowledge, to ask questions about what is being done, to what end, why and how. If it is assumed too soon that it is clear what it is all about, then dialogue can quickly degenerate into an exchange of views about how to deal with reality. Discussion then rises above concrete problems and drifts into the ideal world.

In a learning organization it is a matter of obtaining a consensus about how a concrete problem can be solved. It is not a matter of obtaining a consensus about what the world should ideally look like. This game is a favourite one in prescriptive organizations and serves to while away the time and mete out each other's powers under the banner of 'policy-making'.

Learning is always related to the task, work and the problem. That prevents discussions from wandering. Not in order to lecture or punish each other thereby or to cover oneself, but in order to learn from each other.

In this process, questions are generally simple but at the same time awkward. Who exactly are our customers and consumers? What is the product we are selling them and what do we know about them?

9.6 MULTILATERAL LEARNING

A learning organization is an organization which learns multilaterally. 'Multilateral' here indicates all levels of learning: rules, insights and principles. A learning organization is designed so that there are sufficient differences to keep the

dialogue at all these levels of learning – rules, insights and principles – going and open. The norm for the question 'to what extent is difference desirable?' here lies in the variability of the environment in which the organization operates. The organization must be varied enough to respond to variety in its surroundings. Here Ashby's law applies: 'Only variety can beat variety'.
A characteristic feature of a learning organization is then *variety*. Variety exists in:

- people: thinkers alongside doers, reflecters alongside deciders, individualists and team players, technically oriented alongside commercially oriented;
- strategies: planned rational strategies alongside pragmatic intuitive strategies;
- structures: simple lines alongside complex matrices;
- cultures: task culture alongside individual culture, role culture alongside power culture;
- systems: complex alongside simple, systems for action and systems for reflection.

A learning organization consciously permits *contradictions* and *paradoxes*. In a learning organization conflicts are not seen as threats to be avoided but as challenges to be met, with the goal of stimulating on-going debate on rules, insights and principles. People want to keep on learning at single-, double- and triple-loop level in order to maintain vitality and constantly develop.
This is where the learning organization diverges from all previous types. In the entrepreneurial organization, learning is directed towards doing: ability and courage. The unlearning organization is primarily concerned with unlearning. The prescriptive organization is a combination of unilateral learning components.
The greatest paradox with the learning organization is that one has to be prescriptive on the meta-level in order to keep the organization a learning one, especially where the handling of learning principles is concerned.
A learning organization is not paradise. Learning together and agreeing on the above-mentioned principles is burdensome,

difficult and sometimes also very painful. All the learning organizations we know of have to expend a great deal of effort to sustain their learning. On the one hand, there is the temptation to sink into the calm and security of the prescriptive organization. On the other hand is the threat of the collapse of the organization.

If a learning organization is to be kept a learning one, one thing must, paradoxically enough, be above discussion: the desire to remain a learning organization. The desire to continue learning and seeking debate is the key to the organization's identity.

9.7 LEARNING TO LEARN

Learning in a learning organization is directed towards developing the potential for learning to learn: *meta-learning.* The basis for this potential is self-knowledge; in particular knowledge about how and why you are learning and wish to learn. One of the main reasons why crises in entrepreneurial and prescriptive organizations so often end up with the avoidance of problems is that people know themselves so badly; they are not aware of their own collective competences and incompetences and do not have the courage or the will to look at these.

This demands collective potential, the courage and the will to look at yourself in an orderly manner, which is different from being self-absorbed. It involves detached observation and analysis of your own collective functioning, which requires the art of knowing how to stand outside yourself. But even more than potential this requires courage, because what you see in the mirror can sometimes be painfully hard. Finally, it requires above everything the will to draw back at set times from everyday activities and worries.

A learning organization is based on a philosophy in which its members consider themselves and each other as adults: as people who have the will and the courage to take on responsibility for their own functioning in relation to the other person, and who expect the same of the other person.

Becoming a Learning Organization

The medium is the message.

McLuhan

10.1 WHY BECOME A LEARNING ORGANIZATION?

Never before in history have so many companies seen themselves confronted with so many and such rapid changes in their environment. Change has become the rule. Many articles and books have already appeared, describing these changes from a variety of angles. We summarize here only the most significant consequences of changes for the organization.

- Companies have less and less time in which to build up carefully planned organizations.
- Radical changes are taking place in working processes due to progressive automation and information structures.
- In growth areas there is increasing emphasis on research, development, service and consultancy.
- The significant increase in the level of education combined with the tendency towards individualization means that people are beginning to make different demands on cooperation.
- Individual and collective competences acquired become out of date at an ever increasing rate.

Both the opportunities and the threats with which organizations are confronted from the environment are increasing; in number, intensity and influence. Entrepreneurial organizations look like being able to profit from these, but they also threaten to become their football. So long as it is a question of more of the same, they are able to adapt without really understanding the process. If it is a question of doing things differently it suddenly becomes clear that learning potential is very limited.

It is much more troublesome for prescriptive organizations. It is these organizations, with their consistent emphasis on improving efficiency, that we largely have to thank for our welfare. But at the same time this emphasis on efficiency has led to their becoming unwieldy, prescriptive systems which are hardly capable of adapting to the environment, taking up opportunities and averting threats. Many of these organizations need to adopt a new form of organization. An organization which has the features of a learning organization.

10.2 HOW TO BECOME A LEARNING ORGANIZATION

As described in Chapter 7, changes in a prescriptive organization usually occur as follows: initially we plan, with or without a lot of participation, as accurate a blueprint as possible of the desired organization in terms of strategy, structure, culture and systems. Then we begin to introduce the blueprint and teach everyone how to act in accordance with it.

This approach could be called a *tourist model*: first we establish as precisely as possible where we want to go and how to get there, and then we set off. The consequence of this approach is that a subsequent dichotomy is formed between the process of reorganization and the process of behavioural change, wherein the process of reorganization determines the content of behavioural change and how it is to take place.

In a nutshell: think first and act later.

In a learning organization changes come about according to the *trekker model*: even though we do not know precisely where we are heading and certainly not where we will finish up, we choose a direction and off we go.

In this sort of approach the processes of reorganization and behavioural change are integrated. Behavioural and organizational change take place in a common, collective learning process in which thought, actions, reflections and decisions interchange with each other. Behavioural change leads to organizational change, which in turn stimulates further behavioural change. The new organization is not the *cause* of a learning process, as in the tourist model, but its *result*.

Our opinion now is that when a prescriptive organization wishes to make the transition to a learning organization, the trekker model, which begins with collective behavioural change, should be chosen, that is, it should begin with learning, because learning is behavioural change. Start with doing rather than with thinking.

The first argument in favour of the trekker model is obviously a very pragmatic argument: time. Changes are coming faster and faster, so fast that there is hardly enough time to establish first direction and destination precisely. By the time the blueprint of the desired situation has been planned, the environment has already changed again. Furthermore this pragmatic-looking argument is also one of the most fundamental causes of the crisis in contemporary bureaucracies.

The second argument for choosing the trekker model is that the tourist model is the favourite model of the prescriptive organization. If you wish to make fundamental changes you must choose a medium other than the usual one: '*The medium is the message*'. In prescriptive organizations the organization in the instrumental sense is used as a means of control. Strategy, structure, culture and systems are seen in those organizations as prescribing instruments for imposing behaviour and behavioural change. If you then also wish to achieve a different organization, in the institutional sense, using the same instruments, that only provides the reasons for setting up a new prescriptive organization.

A third argument for the trekker model is that strategies, structures, cultures and systems are not in fact instruments for bringing about change, but rather for maintaining continuity.

10.3 CHANGE VERSUS CONTINUITY

A central dilemma of management is finding a balance between *continuity* and *change*. Every business ultimately earns its daily bread through primary processes. These must be continued at all costs. At the same time, parts of these processes need to be adapted at certain times, and sometimes almost continually, to the demands of the environment. Now the main function of strategy, structure, systems and culture is to *support* the existing current processes, that is to say, support continuity. This is almost true by definition; sociologists often define structure and culture as congealed behaviour. Is it then not illogical to use these same instruments to initiate and guide change?

In Chapter 7 we described the friction which can arise between the processes of reorganization and behavioural change, caused by the fact that changes in structure and system do not run parallel to changes in behaviour. That alone gives cause for thought about the efficiency of these instruments as means of control. It is probably one of the most important reasons why reorganizations often have so little effect and the working processes usually settle back into their old ways after reorganization.

We are the first to admit that some changes, especially those dictated by technology, are not possible other than via the changing of structures and systems. However, we are concerned here with the autonomous decision to become a learning organization. Then one must use the organization (in the instrumental sense) as it was intended, namely to support desired behaviour, and not to change it.

In practice this can even mean that in the initial phase of collective behavioural change those existing systems or structures which oppose the desired behaviour are temporarily suspended. They are only reintroduced in a modified form when the new, desired level of competence has been reached, with the aim of sustaining this new level. In the literature on quality improvement, this is sometimes called *safeguarding*.

10.4 LEADERSHIP VERSUS MANAGEMENT

Good leadership is a critical success factor for any organization. This applies all the more to an organization undergoing change. For an organization wishing to make the transition to a learning organization, this is even a decisive factor. The decisive element there is primarily not what management says or thinks but what it does. What people do can be discerned primarily from the behaviour they demonstrate and the means they employ.

Managing, that is, motivating people towards the desired behaviour can, as we stated in Chapter 2, be carried out in two ways, namely *indirectly*, by means of strategies, structures, systems and culture – that is what we call management – and *directly*, by means of persuasion, supporting, advising and motivating – that is what we call leadership. The transition of an organization to a learning organization does not so much require management as *leadership*; direct personal influencing of people. And it should begin with leadership at the top. The most important demand that must be made on leaders is that they, in the behaviour that they demonstrate and in the means that they use, show that they are also prepared to learn. Here too, the medium is the 'message'.

The first stage in the transition to a learning organization is then to ensure that leaders of this sort are appointed to the crucial positions.

Leading Collective Learning Processes

> What would happen if each echelon of a
> hierarchy were required to earn back at
> least its share of the total costs?

Managing changes means providing leadership for collective learning processes at all levels.

Every complex working association should be analysed as an entity of mutually comprehensive systems. A factory consists of departments, but is, itself, a subsection of a division. The division, in its turn, is part of a concern. One system contains another, like a set of Russian dolls. The smallest independent unit is the system, which, in principle, could stand on its own outside the organizational association. Each system requires three management functions, which must be fulfilled in order to guarantee continuity and to change the system when necessary.

The first function is the managing of the operational process. At this level the fluctuations deriving from the environment which have an effect on the operational unit – group, department or division – have to be met. Flows of information must lead to action and involvement in this process in order to guide it in the desired direction. This occurs through amplifying weak signals and softening strong signals. It is information 'in the system' which brings about an *improvement* in the working process. In the first function guidance is given to *single loop* learning processes: learning processes at the *level of rules*.

Deviations in one operational process can affect others 'next door'. A breakdown of the production processes has an impact on the distribution department. This kind of deviation must not only be communicated to colleagues in the neighbouring units but also to the next higher level of management. The function of this second level is to initiate, organize and give direction to dialogue *between* the units, on the basis of collectively agreed goals. In the literature this function is often called *interface management*. To be able to fulfil this function information is necessary about how the whole, the sum of the parts, operates. This information consists of ad hoc messages between sections and systematically gathered audit information; information 'on the system'. Discussion of the insights on which organization is based is generated from such information. Where necessary this brings about learning processes which lead to *renewal*. At the second level guidance is given to *double loop* learning processes: learning processes at the level of *insights*.

To maintain survival the relationship between the whole and the environment must also be managed. This is dealt with by the third function, which initiates, defines and gives direction to the *development* of the whole. Achieving a balance between continuity and change is central to this function. What must be the balance in the organization between the processes which create continuity and the processes in the sphere of development? These development processes cost money, of course, but they are investments for future cash flows. In order to make this kind of evaluation, information about the environment is needed. Questions of being and will may come under discussion as a result of this information. This is also precisely the function of 'mission statements' and 'business definitions'. They express what sort of business it wishes to be or become. This third level function guides *triple loop* learning processes: learning processes at the level of *development*.

Three levels of learning process are found in all systems which are capable of survival. They may differ in range, depth and time scale. *Range* refers to horizontal extent of decisions made, *depth* to the vertical extent and *time scale* to the time for which they apply.

For a proper understanding of it, it should be noted that 'level', in this context, is not synonymous with 'hierarchy'. All managers fulfil all three of the functions. When intervening in the relationship *between* the smelting works and the foundry, the works manager of a steel factory is fulfilling a second-level

Learning loop	Learning area	Learning level	Learning result	Management functions
Single	**rules**	obligation & permission	improvement	first level
	+	+		
Double	**insights**	knowledge & understanding	renewal	second level
	+	+		
Triple	**principles**	courage & will	development	third level

Figure 13 Organizational change.

function. Intervention *in* the smelting works itself is a first, operational-level function. If the works manager takes part in management team deliberations on the strategic positioning of the steel factory, this represents a third-level management function. For the directors concerned, however, these discussions are second-level management functions, and so on.

The three essential functions recur at each level of department, business unit, company and division, except that at each level, the range, depth and time scale are of a higher order.

The three essential functions thus correspond to the three levels of the learning processes.

Related single, double and triple loop processes can therefore appear at the same time in all sorts of divergent sections of the organization and at all sorts of different levels. Whether and when a combination and coordination of these separate processes is necessary depends on how interdependent the various units, companies and divisions are. However, the more radical the learning process is in its progression from rules to insights and from insights to principles, the greater the need also becomes to link it with other learning processes. There is, for example, a greater need to cooperate with comparable departments for a personnel department considering its role as line supervisor – 'do we wish to control or support?' – a triple loop learning process, than for a technical service department which is revising its data files.

Part 3
Organizational Education

This part of the book concerns the education of organizations. In the light of our definition of education this means helping with organizational learning. Given our definition of learning this, in turn, means helping with the changing of organizational behaviour. By helping, we mean goal-conscious educational intervention, in the form of specifically designed programmes, to which we shall ascribe the name *organizational courses*. We mean by organizational courses a coherent series of interventions into an organizational learning process.

Our attention is focused particularly on what we describe as *learning* organizational courses, which contrast with *prescriptive* organizational courses.

This distinction runs parallel with that made in Part Two between learning and prescriptive organizations, and it applies specifically to divergences in outlook on organizational change. As we stated in Part Two, in a prescriptive organization organizational change is defined as a change of structure, strategy, culture or systems. It is a type of organizational change which ultimately imposes a change in behaviour.

Organizational courses which support this learning process imposed by organizational change are prescriptive courses.

The roles are reversed in a learning organization. An organizational change is not the cause of a learning process, but the outcome. Organizational learning runs parallel with organizational change. Organizational courses which support this kind of process of change are learning courses.

In Chapter 12, we state what are the most important features of an organizational course. In particular we examine the connection between education, training, forming and consulting. Various forms of organizational course are reviewed, in passing. It will be seen that several forms make the unjustified claim that they are organizational courses, while other forms, which do not tend to be seen as such, are indeed so. The actual form of many organizational courses alone also makes it evident that they are prescriptive courses.

In this book we concentrate on only one type of organizational course, namely the educational course which has as its goal *to help organizations*, particularly prescriptive organizations, *to take the first step in becoming a learning organization*. Of great importance in making a good start to an organizational course is the setting up beforehand of a learning contract with all the parties concerned – the instigator, educational staff and participants – so that it is clear for all parties what is expected of each other. This is what we call the *contract phase*. In Chapter 13, we describe the most significant activities which the project leader, who takes primary responsibility for drawing up and handling this contract, must carry out in this phase.

In Chapter 14, we deal with the second phase, the planning phase, in which interventions are prepared and sequenced on the basis of the questions of when should which intervention be made and why.

Chapter 15 concerns the *implementation phase*. In this chapter, we discuss the different stages that occur during the implementation and the salient features of each stage.

Collective learning is a *paradoxical* process, and in Chapter 16 we explore some of the various paradoxes, and their consequences for the learning process and the possible educational interventions.

We conclude this part with a look back at these questions: what does the education of organizations comprise, and what is the role of the educator or the adviser in it? The position which is defended there is that there is no longer any difference between an educator and an adviser.

Features of an Educational Course

> Often those who become teachers are eager to
> dominate but not sufficiently competent to do
> that to adults.
>
> *Bertrand Russell*

12.1 COMBINING EDUCATION AND TRAINING

As we stated in Part 1, a learning process is a cyclic process of thinking, doing, reflecting and deciding. While this is true of individual learning, it is even more so for a collective learning process, a process of organizational learning.

Now, an organizational course is a series of interventions in this learning cycle, interventions which differ in type according to whether it is a question of help with thinking, doing, reflecting or deciding. It is a combination of education in the narrower sense, training, forming and consulting: a series of interventions linked together by the problem which prompted the beginning of the learning process. In this chapter, we will argue that an organizational learning process which does not run through all the phases of the learning cycle will either become a non-committal or prescriptive process, or will remain at the level of single loop, or at best double loop learning.

The two most familiar forms of organizational education programme are the *organizational education course* (in the narrower sense of education) and the *organizational training course*. Many of the so-called in-company or tailor-made programmes fall into the first category. As forms of collective education they are relatively recent, whereas organizational training courses are much older.

A characteristic feature of prescriptive organizations is that training courses and educational courses are often separate programmes, and are aimed at different target groups. Lower and middle managers tend to be sent to training courses, learning to do; indeed, *training is helping to do*. Participants learn to communicate more effectively, to solve problems and to deal with conflict. The attention to knowledge and insight is minimal. The principal activity is practising. A recent exception to this is provided by the educational courses formed under the aegis of quality improvement, where in quality circles learning focuses not only on doing, but also on thinking.

By contrast, in courses for higher and top management the emphasis is entirely on increasing knowledge and insight; and thus on education in the narrower sense: *education is helping to think*. When these courses do work with skills, for example, analysing case studies (preferably cases from other companies), the skills are restricted to dealing with concepts and theories. In other words, they are skills at the level of talk theory. Attention to personal skills at the level of action theory is virtually taboo for this target group. It is evidently assumed that collective competence in this area can be taken for granted at the top. The reality, however, appears to be different.

It is essential for learning and certainly also for collective learning to experiment in practice, in the real world, and to try out what has been conceived at the thinking level, in theory. With exclusively training-oriented courses, learning is restricted at best to the learning of adroitness, 'the trick'. It is learning at the single loop level. With exclusively education-oriented courses, learning is restricted to the increase or improvement of knowledge. However, double loop learning can only take place if such insights are linked with adaptation to real practical problems.

The first feature of an effective learning organization course, is that education is combined with training in one and the same programme.

12.2 COMBINING EDUCATION AND TRAINING WITH FORMING

Forming is helping to reflect.
Early in the 1970s forming was a popular educational intervention in the business world. At that time, there were various forming programmes, some of which were specifically directed towards collective learning, including, among others, the so-called family, group and team-building sessions. From around the second half of the 1970s, this sort of programme fell into disrepute for all sorts of, often justified, reasons. Currently, however, forming programmes are experiencing a comeback, under the name of outward bound training courses and survival programmes. Such courses are, for the time being, primarily aimed at developing individual, personal qualities. As an intervention in an organizational learning process, 'forming' (a rather inaccurate term, in fact) is still a poorly adapted and not widely accepted way of assisting learning. In a process of organizational learning, and especially in a learning process which is supposed to be a step on the way towards becoming a learning organization, reflection is an indispensable and significant moment. It is pre-eminently the moment for learning collectively how to learn collectively. Indeed, as we stated in Section 3.5, learning to learn requires the ability and, above all, the courage to stand back and examine with detachment your own version of reality. In other words, without forming, a process of organizational learning remains at best a double loop learning process, and can never become a triple loop learning process.

A second feature of an effective learning organization educational course is that an essential part of it must be forming: holding up mirrors, feedback about unconscious realities, collective behavioural models, blind spots, fantasies, assumptions, perceptions and so on.

At the same time, though, forming interventions need to be linked with training and education. Forming as a separate, independent intervention is of little effect. Reflection is an activity dominated by feeling and it has little impact if it is not linked to thought, an activity dominated by reason. Thinking in its turn has little effect if it is not combined with action and connected to feeling.

12.3 COMBINING EDUCATION, TRAINING AND FORMING WITH ADVISING

One of the most frequent and often most effective types of collective learning is what is commonly known as a *work conference*. These conferences have the goal of making decisions. Managers step back for several days in order to make collective decisions on matters such as:

- mission, business definition, product portfolios or marketing strategies;
- starting points for a new organizational structure, or the repositioning of the department or division;
- agreements about mutual task and role distribution, or form of cooperation.

An adviser or consultant is often called in to lead or assist in the running of such conferences. We usually also call this kind of assistance *advising*.

Advising is helping with deciding.
Curiously enough, one seldom hears reference to learning or education at these conferences. It is all the more curious because one of the most radical forms of collective learning takes place in this context: learning the collective competence of making decisions with each other; decisions about collectively shared rules, insights or principles as a phase in a process of single, double or triple loop learning.

The point that we wish to make is clear: deciding is an inseparable part of the process of reflecting, thinking and doing. To put it differently, doing, reflecting and thinking have little point if they are not connected to a moment of decision.

Put in the educator's terms: training, forming and education will not have much effectiveness if they do not also include advising.

Processes of organizational learning and education which lack this moment of decision or advice always run the risk of two great dangers. Either the courses will be non-committal – if no agreements are made there is no obligation to apply what has been learned – or the courses will become prescriptive, which occurs when someone other than the participants has decided what has to be learned and why.

12.4 THE PROBLEM AS A LINK

One reason for changing an organization and thus beginning a process of organizational learning is that present organizational behaviour now or in the near future can or will no longer deliver the desired result. The difference between the present and the desired situation is what we call a *problem*.

Now, the problem which gives rise to a learning process and, by extension, to an organizational course, both determines the goal of the course and its content and also its participants. It will be clear, given the fact that a course is considered necessary, that we are concerned with a deep-seated problem with which many others are connected: a syndrome. Hence we often speak of the *core problem*.

The *goal* of an organizational learning process is to solve an organizational problem, described either in the negative sense, that is to say, in terms of the undesired effects of present behaviour, or, and even preferably, in the positive sense, that is to say, in terms of the effects desired in the future. Indeed, goal and problem are two sides of the same coin: a goal is a reciprocal formulation of a problem. A few examples can explain this point.

At the moment, 50% of our turnover is obtained from the sale of hardware, 30% from software and 20% from advisory services; if we wish to maintain our turnover this situation will have to be reversed within five years.

In our company there is disagreement between business units and head office over the question of what is decided centrally and what is decentralized; the goal is to reach a series of agreements on vertical cooperation which delivers optimum synergy.

One year ago, we entered into a merger with the purpose of integrating activities; however, cooperation is just not getting off the ground.

Our product portfolio is, in many people's view, unbalanced; we are aiming for a portfolio which will guarantee us a good long-term cash flow.

Signals from the market indicate that we are lumping our clients together too much; if we want to be sure of our share of the market we should probably aim at greater segmentation.

Through the death of our owner–director we are at the moment working
aimlessly; we should like to get straightened out.

By *content* we mean what the participants need in terms of
collective knowledge, insights, skills and attitudes, in order to
solve the problem. The difference between participants' actual
and required competence is critical in determining the content
of a course.

So, the problem which prompted the learning process dictates
not only the *purpose* of learning, but also *what* must be learned:
the viewpoints, concepts and theories, the methods and
techniques, the mirrors and practice situations which need to be
included in the programme. The timing of different sorts of
intervention – education, training, forming or advising – is
determined by the problem solving phase.

The problem acts as a link; as a bond between education
training, forming and advising, another reason for speaking of a
core problem.

Furthermore, the problem is the driving force behind
participation in the learning process or the course. Those people
who have taken part in the problem *and* in the solution of it
must participate.

Considering that problems seldom draw upon formal or
informal organizational dividing lines, this means that in
practice people from different levels of the hierarchy nearly
always participate in organizational courses: people from
different departments, line and staff; people from different
disciplines, with different responsibilities and powers and with
different competences.

It is a question of setting up a group to which the instigator of
the course, on the basis of the position, competence and
involvement of the participants, entrusts the job of approaching
the problem by learning and thereby changing the organization.

12.5 LEARNING VERSUS PRESCRIPTIVE COURSES

Companies may decide to send their staff, usually starting with
their managers, to an organizational course in order to make
them take cognizance of new concepts, theories and methods,
with the intention (or the assumption or at any rate in the hope)
that this will induce them to carry out changes in the

organization. However, no occasions are included in this course when collective decisions are made about what is to be changed and how. There is a very great chance that the course will to a great extent have a *non-committal* character. Learning will then be restricted to the individual and never reach the level of collective learning.

Even more often, a company will send people to a course because they wish to bring about reorganization or because they already have reorganized. The purpose of the course is to give the participants a more detailed explanation of the why and how of the reorganization and/or to exercise them in the intended new behaviour – in short, persuasion and instruction, with the goal of adaptation and conformity with the new organization. The course then becomes a prescriptive course and cannot fail to produce a prescriptive organization as its end result. People learn collectively to understand and to be able, but not to want. That side of things has already been thought out and decided by someone else.

Many of the requests for courses we have received over the years were, certainly with hindsight, of the type: 'Help us to develop a learning organization by means of a prescriptive course'. A request that is not feasible, because it is impossible by definition. The content of the course is then in conflict with the form. However, we took up these requests several times because the contradictory aspects of such requests are not always easy to discern, either by the person asking, or by those intending to help. We fell into the trap, so to speak. Some examples make the point.

Our managers are so reluctant to change. Could you teach them (usually 'tell' is what is meant) that they must be more flexible, to take more initiative and pay less attention to the rules?

We have decided to decentralize decision-making to a large extent... . Could you explain to our managers that this means that they will have to... (there follows a summary of what they must and must not do).

Our commercial people do not think strategically enough... . Could you explain to them that strategic thinking means that you must... (another summary).

Our divisional directors are not people managers... they really ought much more to... . Could you not teach them these things?

We once had the experience of being asked by a board of directors to develop this type of programme, but it was spelled out that not a drop of alcohol was to be imbibed before 10 p.m., everyone was to be in bed by 1 a.m. and at least 12 hours' work had to be done per day. These were contradictory requests rather like: 'Be spontaneous' or, even better, 'Be mature'.

The salient feature of a *learning course* is that ultimately it is the participants who decide *what* has to be learned: the *learning content*. The starting point is the *problem* which gives rise to the learning process. The instigator – board of directors, directors, management team – only dictates the *wherefore* of learning: the *learning goal*. And again, by 'learning goal' we therefore mean the (positive) formulation of the problem. In other words, the instigator places a problem before the learning group instead of talking to them about a solution. That is an adult approach. An approach furthermore which does justice to the function of each level of management to be found within a learning organization (see Chapter 10). It is conceivable that participants will redefine the problem or find new problems during the course. Then renewed discussion of it takes place with decision-making by the instigator. Establishing what kind of help is expected from the project leader should be a matter for discussion between project leader, instigator and participants: it should be the result of a collectively agreed contract.

In our experience, the instigators of courses are seldom at variance with the view we have sketched. Internal trainers or those responsible for management development often oppose participants' influence on the content. They have the tendency either to ask the instigator for instructions on the content of the course (often wrongly described by trainers as learning goals), or to decide on the content themselves. They think that it is their job to know and decide on what the participants need.

However skilfully the above dichotomy between goal and content and the associated decision-making is dealt with, one cannot prevent conflicts arising between the goals of individual participants and those of the organization, especially where collective learning and education processes are concerned. There are almost always participants who are, and who also during the course remain, at variance with the definition of the problem (the learning goal) in the first instance formulated by the instigator and, in the second instance, taken over or redefined by the participants. However, that is not an educational problem and it is certainly not a problem for the course leaders to deal with. It has nothing to do with the dilemma of learning in freedom and learning in captivity, or with the dilemma of a learning versus a prescriptive approach. It is a personal problem transcending this for the participant concerned, revolving around the question: do I wish to work for and with an organization whose goals I do not share?

Even if all the participants agree about the problem and make their decision on learning content – considering the fact that it is a matter of a collective learning process – conflicts can still arise between individual and collective interests. Becoming collectively competent does not in fact imply that each individual is or has to be equally competent. On the contrary, the whole point is that individuals contribute to the collective according to their competence. One of the most penetrating aspects of this mutual learning with and from each other is appraising and positioning each other and yourself in relation to this competence. However, that is not an equally pleasant process for everyone.

12.6 COLLECTIVE LEARNING FOR COLLECTIVE CHANGE

In this chapter we have defined an organizational course as a series of coherent interventions into a collective learning process. The interventions will take the form of education, training, forming or consultancy depending on the phase in which the process of thinking, doing, reflecting or deciding is taking place.

Here it may be a case of a learning process of years or it may be a learning process of only a few months. It may be a process which requires relatively little help in the form of a course. On the other hand we know learning processes in which the support of an educational course is sought again at least once a quarter.

In short, little can be said in general terms about organizational courses other than to mention a number of general distinguishing features to be found in them. Among other things it depends on the type and scope of the problem, the duration of the learning process, the participants and the help needed.

In the following chapters of this book we shall examine

organizational courses whose goal it is to help organizations take the first step in the direction of a learning organization: courses which help organizations to change while learning. These are by definition learning courses.

In this sort of course, therefore, the rules and insights and the principles of the organization come under discussion at the same time; it is a question of learning at three levels at once. To achieve this, outside help is necessary. These courses can practically never be run successfully by the company's own education department, for the simple reason that this is itself part of the company and as such it is formed by the very rules, insights and principles which the course aims to discuss.

For almost everyone who has grown up with a prescriptive organization, a view in which organizational change is synonymous with collective learning is so new that they can hardly imagine it. It is a way of learning which in itself needs to be learned, and that is the primary aim of this kind of educational course: helping organizations to change as they learn; to learn how to learn.

The Contract Phase

People always get what they ask for. The trouble
is only that before they get it, they never know
what in fact they asked for.

Aldous Huxley

13.1 THE CONTRACT PARTNERS

This phase is often referred to in literature as the intake phase.
Its aim is to arrive at agreement between the parties involved on
the goals and content of the organizational course, and this is
why we prefer to speak of the contract phase.

The three main parties involved in the creation of this kind of
contract are:

- The *instigator*, that is, the person who decides whether or
  not to embark on a course, chooses which educational
  institution to bring in and – most importantly – defines the
  goal of the course.
- The *participants*, who take part in the course and who, as
  stated above, ultimately decide on the course content.
- The *educational staff*, who design and carry out the course.
  Initially we shall not refer to the staff, but to the project
  leader, that is, the leader of the staff. In the first phase it is
  usually the project leader who, in the name of the staff, is
  responsible for relations with the other parties. He or she is
  also the person who is responsible for the creation and
  maintenance of the contract.

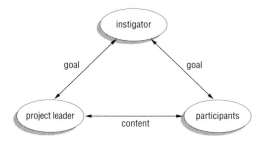

Figure 14 The contract partners.

This chapter is therefore also written from the point of view of the project leader assuming that it is an external project leader. Firstly, we deal with the contract between instigator and project leader (Sections 13.2–13.4); then the contract between instigator and participants and between project leader and participants (Section 13.5). Alongside the three main parties, other people often play a part, such as sponsors, internal project leaders and so on. We reserve comment on these until Section 13.7.

13.2 THE INITIAL CONTRACT BETWEEN PROJECT LEADER AND INSTIGATOR

The most essential contract is that between project leader and instigator. It determines, to a large extent, the other contracts. At this point we come up directly against a serious problem. This contract needs to be concluded at a time when the project leader knows very little about the organization and can therefore very easily fall into traps. Even more perilous, the first trap is set for the very first contact, because, after all, who is the instigator?

Initial contact with an external educational institute, if it is a case of management courses, is almost always made by the head of management development (MD). If lower or middle management is involved, then it is usually the head of education (E). If the heads of MD or E have grown up within a prescriptive organization, there is a high probability that they hold the following ideas among others:

- That they are the instigators, or at least the delegated instigators;
- That the project belongs to their department, or, in crude terms, that they can 'score' or 'fail';
- That their department determines – naturally in consultation, but it does so nevertheless – what themes are on the agenda of the course and who takes part.

The project leader's first task is to make it clear, without the department head running away immediately, that none of these ideas is valid in an organizational course:

- That it is not the department but the participants who determine the content of the course;
- That the project does not belong to their department, but to the department(s) where the problem occurs;
- That the course could involve participants from several hierarchical levels, thus including levels that come outside the sphere of MD or E;
- Above all, that they can never be the instigators (unless of course the problem is in their own department), and that they therefore do not determine the goal of the course.

The instigator is the person who takes responsibility for tackling the problem that gives rise to the start of a process of organizational learning. In a course for higher management, this is nearly always at the level of director or of the board of managment. It is vitally important for the project leader to establish early contact with the instigator. Such contact, however, can often only be made through the heads of MD or E, who often consider themselves to be the instigators. Bypassing seldom or never makes any sense. So the only way forward for the (external) project leader is to persuade the heads of the correctness of the above views and only then to conclude a contract with them regarding their mutual relationship. In Section 13.7 we look at this issue in more detail. One should also bear in mind how long and tiresome the route to the instigator can be if the first contact is not the heads of departments but one of their colleagues.

Once the project leader has penetrated as far as the instigator, problems can recur if the instigator is of the same frame of mind:

'But I delegated this responsibility to the head of MD'. The question also repeats itself: 'Who is the instigator?' Can the whole matter be assigned to the member of the board with the portfolio for personnel matters? If the course involves the whole organization, once again the answer must be: no. The instigator must then be the whole board, not one individual member.

The next problem is to explain to the instigator that task setting is not required from them in terms of what participants ought to know, understand, be able to do or want to do, but merely in terms of a problem to be dealt with. With this a mandate is also requested to entrust the solution of the problem to the participants (and the project leader as helper). As mentioned in the previous chapter, trainers (heads of MD or E) often have greater difficulty with this standpoint than directors or the board of management, provided of course that the latter have confidence in the project leader and especially in his or her attitude. The above position of the project leader is only credible if the same project leader demonstrates through behaviour and attitude that the role as 'agent' of the instigator has been understood and demonstrates a willingness to play this role: namely helping to help solve one of the instigator's problems. Only then is the same agent justified in making demands on the instigator, and, if necessary, expressing criticism.

The contract between instigators and project leader is, therefore, not only a contract of content but also a psychological contract: a *contract of trust*. At the same time, the project leader needs to ask for room to verify this contract and to be allowed to consider the initial definition of the problem as a provisional one and be allowed to test this in the organization for correctness, shared nature and *solvability*. Permission must be granted to discuss this freely, with those involved, regardless of their position, opinion or attitude. If instigators will not permit this, or withhold the means, there is little point in continuing. The basis of trust is evidently lacking.

13.3 INVESTIGATION OF CORRECTNESS, SHARED NATURE AND SOLVABILITY OF THE PROBLEM

After the initial contract with the instigator has been agreed, an investigation of the correctness, shared nature and solvability is undertaken.

With regard to *correctness*, two questions are raised: has the problem been formulated correctly and, has the correct problem been formulated? It is not necessary or even possible at this stage to lay a completely correct formulation of the problem on the table. The definition of the problem is generally set aside several times in the course of the learning and educational process. This is inherent to learning. At this stage, it is really a question of finding out if the problem has been formulated with sufficient correctness for the purpose of tackling it collectively.

The more important question is whether the correct problem has been formulated. Organizations are sometimes inclined to plunge collectively into a communally defined problem which is not the real problem. We offer a few examples of this.

> Following the decision to change from a functional to a divisional structure, one of the big questions the company thought it was facing was: how do we divide up the R&D department across all the divisions? On closer examination the real question turned out to be: how can we regulate cooperation at the interfaces between R&D and the divisions?

> After the merger, integration of the two companies did not seem to want to get off the ground. Diagnosis: people did not want to work together. Following a brief investigation, it became clear that a structure had been chosen in which cooperation was not feasible.

> A company decided to implement market segmentation in order to be able to differentiate the provision of services to distinct target groups. On closer analysis it appeared that the problem was not concerned with service but with pricing.

> An instigator complained about lack of creativity, readiness to change and personal initiative among members of his management team. After attending a meeting of the team, the problem turned out to be that the instigator himself was unconsciously intolerant of personal initiative, creativity and the like.

Secondly, an investigation is made into the *shared nature* of the problem; approaching a problem by way of learning and education if the formulation of the problem is agreed upon sufficiently by participants as well as the instigator. If that is not the case, then there is a real danger that the process will descend to the level of a political tug-of-war. Rarely, if ever, will everyone commit themselves completely to the problem formulated. The question then is: what constitutes 'sufficiently'? It is not merely a question of quantity – how many people agree with the formulation of the problem – but also of quality – who agrees with the formulation of the problem. The respect people enjoy by virtue of their formal or informal status is particularly significant in this context.

Once, for example, we carried out an assignment based on a problem formulation to which only the chairman of the board of management subscribed. The other two board members were against it. Conversely, we once did not carry out an assignment because the chairman was against the problem formulation, although the overwhelming majority of the directors were in favour.

A third aspect about which the project leader has to form a judgement, is the *solvability* of the problem. Not every problem lends itself to an approach via a (learning) course route. Even if that is the case, there remains the question of whether a particular organization can proceed in this way. It is, therefore, desirable to evaluate the potential learning capacity and, especially, the readiness of an organization to learn. Do they really wish to proceed in this manner, or is it only confessions of faith at the level of talk theory?

How can the project leader form as quickly as possible such an impression of the organization that he can give an answer to these questions? One could almost write a book about this subject alone. It is essential for the project leader to be aware of the fact that an organization is both a system and a construction. He will have to make a judgement about both:

- the system as it functions on paper: strategy, structure, systems and culture;
- the construction as it is experienced in people's minds; the images, judgements, prejudices and perceptions of the members of the organization.

In addition to written information, discussion with the people involved is also important.

Since the past is a good predictor of the future, it is recommended that the history of the organization be brought into the picture. How were similar problems dealt with in the past? How have advisers been treated? If an organization has a long history of unheeded advice and has dispensed with the services of numerous advisers, this raises questions, especially about learning potential and readiness to learn. The best test of the latter is not so much what is said but what is done. It is then also to be recommended that questions be asked which can only be answered in action, which require a decision and an investment of time or resources.

Already in the contract phase, the project leader must make it quite clear, not just in words but in deeds, that a course in learning is being undertaken. That is to say, during work on defining the problem, the project leader should demonstrate a learning behaviour and a learning attitude and should be prepared over time to change his personal standpoints or set them aside. However, in prescriptive organizations *par excellence* this is often seen as inconsistent, unprofessional, hesitant and inadequate.

The only weapon that the project leader has in this situation is complete openness and intensive dialogue.

13.4 THE FINAL CONTRACT BETWEEN PROJECT LEADER AND INSTIGATOR

The above findings provide a basis for the project leader to suggest to the instigator, for example, that he should take the following steps:

- Introduce changes in the definition of the problem.
- Choose another problem formulation.
- Postpone the project temporarily because a number of fundamental conditions are not adequately fulfilled.
- Abandon the project.

The way in which the instigator reacts to such proposals is another test of the correctness, shared nature and solvability of the problem formulated. If the reaction is defensive or reluctant, a contract is unlikely to be concluded. If the instigator's reactions are actively positive the discussions will result in a definitive contract.

An essential element of this definitive contract is establishing who the participants in the project are to be. As we already stated in the previous chapter, those are the people involved in the problem and in the solution of it. The instigator may, therefore, also be one of them. For a triple loop learning process at the level of the whole organization this is even more certain to be the case. And in that case the instigator therefore also has to be a participant. It is very important that instigators realize they are in fact entrusting the solution of a problem to the participants to be selected by them and they must thus choose those participants to whom they are prepared to give this trust. In this context, there are always two traps awaiting them.

The first is that in trying to avoid conflicts, instigators lack the courage to say 'no' to would-be participants who themselves feel they ought to take part – often for formalistic reasons – when the instigators have no trust in the competence or positive involvement of the persons in question. Sometimes, instigators even let such people take part in the secret hope that negative suspicions will be confirmed during the course, thereby saddling the project leader with what is in fact their problem.

The second trap is that instigators are afraid to say 'yes' to people to whom they do ascribe this competence and involvement but who not (yet) belong to the elite group for which the course was originally planned. This is often for fear of creating precedents.

In both cases, fear of discriminating between individuals and thus undermining the basic norms of a prescriptive organization plays a significant part. Because of this alone, it is particularly important with regard to selection not to make many compromises concerning its basis precisely because the selection of participants is one of the most powerful signals that make clear what is actually intended by the course. It is a signal at the level of doing.

13.5 THE CONTRACT WITH THE PARTICIPANTS

Two contracts come under this heading: between the instigator and the participants and between the educational staff and the participants.

The initiative for the contract between instigator and participants is taken by the instigator. Once again, it is a question of the *goal*, and *wherefore* of the course. When we began setting up this kind of course, we used to advise the instigator to conclude this contract at the actual start of the course, therefore at the beginning of the implementation phase. A step which is then combined with the concluding of the contract between educational staff and participants. Gradually, however, we have begun to advocate concluding the contract between instigator and participants a considerable time before the implementation stage, freeing it from any connection with the contract between staff and participants. This is in order to give participants sufficient time to reflect, so that they do not begin the course with utterly wrong or divergent expectations. It is important to allow the participants room for dialogue with the instigator about anything which is unclear or any possible barriers.

It is also essential to reach as much agreement as possible on the power of decision enjoyed by each party, and when it will be necessary to meet again or to reach decisions, for example, on revision of the definition of the problem or the actions to be undertaken. Both parties must understand that the effect of this contract is not confined to the level of content but that it also applies to relationships. Here, too, we are concerned with a *contract of trust*, the more so as a process is being jointly undertaken, of which no one knows precisely what the end result will be.

The contract between educational staff and participants applies to the staff contribution to the course and thereby the *content* of the course.

Agreements have to be reached on:

- Content-specific interventions: the views, theories and concepts to be introduced.
- Procedural interventions: the methods and techniques to be employed.
- Process-specific interventions: the learning situations to be created; the mirrors to be held up; the way in which this is intended to be accomplished.

Conversely it also concerns agreements on what may be expected of the participants: input, attitude, way of dealing with each other. Here, too, the contract applies to content and relationships. Agreement must be reached on using, correcting or adjusting the contract during the course.

It would be desirable to make a number of these basic agreements before the start of the course. In practice this does not always turn out to be possible, considering that it is a matter not only of a contract with the project leader, although he has primary responsibility, but a contract with the whole staff. In fact this often means that a significant part of the contract with the participants is not finalized at the start of the implementation phase.

13.6 THREE DOUBLE CONTRACTS

Each of the three parties involved thus concludes a double contract:

- instigator with project leader and participants;
- participants with instigator and project leader;
- project leader with instigator and participants.

It is important that all three parties should realize that it is a *three-way contract*, meaning that, for example, participants cannot decide or make judgements unilaterally, or together with the instigator, about the contribution made by the staff. The same holds for the instigator and the project leader, so that project leader and participants cannot together decide on the content of the course independently of the agreed goal set with the task. This is equally true for project leader and instigator.

It is primarily the responsibility of the project leader to ensure that content agreed upon with participants corresponds and continues to correspond with the goals agreed upon with the instigator. If there is a threat of friction or ambiguities between these two, he will have to intervene, possibly by bringing all three parties together again. This must be made clear to all parties in advance, and they must all be willing to commit themselves in word and deed. This renegotiation of the contract is not only important as a means of ensuring a good progression of the learning process, it is also a part of that same learning process. It indicates that the parties are trying to obtain clarity while learning.

The function of these contracts is to make explicit each

person's responsibility, role and contribution: the making of agreements of which people can approve. The creation of clarity is just one of the features of a learning organization. It is as such directly contrary to procedures in prescriptive organizations, which tend to keep this kind of agreement obscure so that, if something goes wrong, the buck can be passed. Success in a prescriptive organization is claimed by many; failure, however, is admitted by none.

13.7 OTHER PARTIES

We have already mentioned that other people, apart from these three parties, often play a role. The most obvious of these is probably the *head of management development* or the *head of the education department*, or their respective representatives. Allocating these roles is at the very least a delicate matter.

The solution we prefer, when possible, is for the head of MD or E – as internal project leader – to share the leadership of the project with the external project leader. However, that is only possible if this person, in the eyes of both the instigator and the participants, has built up an authoritative position – a position which at the same time absolves the external project leader of any possible suspicion of misuse of information obtained during the course. The ambiguous thing about this situation is that the only person that can test this is the external project leader.

Furthermore, internal and external project leaders must be able and willing to treat each other as equal partners, to respect each other's contribution, to give each other room to register results and help each other and/or give a warning if something is not going as desired. If these conditions are not met, this role is not really possible. It will give rise to attempts on both sides to go past each other, or adopt a collision course or blame each other.

Another interested party is the *sponsor*, the person who is paying for the course. Usually instigator and sponsor coincide, but not always. The sponsor is not party to the process. If a sponsor wishes to have a say in the programme, it must be done by influencing the instigator. The counterpart of the sponsor is the director of the educational institute, who is also not directly involved. His role is to observe at a distance whether the project leader is acting with the other two parties, instigators and participants, in accordance with the principles underlying a learning organization.

One last party is the *educational staff*. Particularly with larger projects a considerable number of lecturers, (senior) professors, trainers and guest speakers may be involved. It is essential that these outside speakers, at any rate where they play a key role, should subscribe to the philosophy underlying learning organizational courses and that they are able to deal with the approach deriving from it. Unfortunately, it must be said that the number of (senior) professors among them is small. Even they have been brought up in a prescriptive tradition, and one of the responsibilities of the project leader is to recruit staff capable of providing a learning course. If they lack this ability, the project leader will have to teach it to them, a task which is often at least as difficult as concluding a good contract.

The Planning Phase

At the moment of planning you must take your
plan seriously, otherwise you can't take yourself
seriously. At the moment of implementation
precisely the opposite is true.

14.1 THE GOAL OF THE PLANNING PHASE

The goal is to develop an organizational course plan. We have
consciously chosen the word 'plan', firstly because we are not
speaking of a timetable stating at what time which lecturer is
addressing which topic, and secondly in order to indicate the
uncertain, unpredictable progression of an organizational
course. We have never experienced an organizational course
which turned out precisely according to plan. We would even go
so far as to say that if it does, the learning process has probably
not been good and that, consciously or unconsciously, the plan
has been misused by staff or participants to avoid sticking points
and difficulties.

It is even better to assume in advance that the course will
indeed turn out differently from what was planned. This
increases staff awareness of what is actually happening and
creates the flexibility necessary to make those interventions
which appear adequate at that moment, even if they had not
been planned in advance. It also means that it is sensible to
prepare additional interventions besides the planned ones, just
in case.

By 'course plan' we mean a sequentially ordered series of
interventions – content specific, process specific and procedural – which the staff undertakes to make during the
learning process.

The primary function of this kind of plan is to work out *which* possible interventions can or could be made, *when* and *why*.

14.2 CONTENT-SPECIFIC INTERVENTIONS

Here, it is a question of planning the content of the concepts, theories and models which are to be offered and planning the form they are to take: lectures, summarizing sessions, literature and film. As preparation for these interventions the staff should try to form an image of the problem or problems which gave rise to the course, together with the relevant context of these problems, in this case the organization. In order to be able to plan these interventions it will be necessary to hold interviews, collect and read through internal reports and memos and go through relevant literature.

By 'staff' we mean the project leader plus any lecturers who may be responsible for the content-specific interventions, with the term 'lecturers' also including experts from within the company who may be called upon in the course.

It is important that staff focus on the *problem* and not on the possible solution(s) to it, as subject-centred lecturers are very inclined to do. An orientation is required which opens up the various points of view and interpretations, the relevant combinations and aspects, backgrounds and motives. The aim of this is to select and present concepts and theories which can help the participants to analyse and define the problem themselves, and to develop alternative solutions.

The educational staff must resist the temptation to define the problem themselves; this is the job of the participants. Becoming aware of everyone's, often very different, viewpoint, interpretation and opinion of the problem is often itself one of the most important stages of collective learning. For this reason we do not advocate working with case studies designed by the educational staff in advance, since every case study, however generally it is written, already contains an interpretation of the problem definition. It is far more instructive to make the cases explicit in the minds of the participants.

14.3 PROCESS-SPECIFIC INTERVENTIONS

This section is concerned with planning interventions into the process of cooperation. These interventions aim to give insight into the functional and dysfunctional aspects of the cooperation pattern and the underlying mechanisms and motives. With organizational courses in particular, process-specific interventions are often at least as important as content-specific interventions. If companies are having difficulty learning, that is to say, they lack the potential to approach their problems, this is often only partly attributable to content-specific deficiencies. Especially in prescriptive organizations there is often an superfluity of knowledge and insights distributed among individual members. Difficulties are much more likely to be the result of the collective inability to bring together this individual knowledge and insight effectively and to convert it into decisions and of the inability to cooperate while learning. Inability is not only determined by individual knowledge and ability, but also by collective agreements, both explicit and implicit, about what is *permitted* or *not permitted* or what *must be done*. Such agreements can lead to a steady diminution of the courage to act, and this leads in the long run to collective incompetence.

The preparation for process-specific interventions consists predominantly in observing cooperative behaviour within the organization, for example, by attending meetings or holding individual or especially group interviews. There is an even greater danger here of wanting to investigate too much, than in preparing for content-specific interventions. For the educational staff it is thus the art of restricting themselves to what is relevant and necessary. Once again, this is determined by the problem or problems for which the course was set up. It is really a question of building up a picture of the aspects of the cooperation process which stand in the way of approaching the problem properly, or – to put it differently – which might lead to the problem being avoided.

In the first instance it is a matter of recognizing this evasion behaviour – of recognizing behaviour where people are acting 'as if' they were solving problems, but are actually avoiding them. This sort of behaviour often finds expression in fight-or-flight behaviour, pairing and dependency. Secondly, it is a question of gaining a picture of *what* is being avoided or overlooked. Once this impression has been gained, along with some ideas about possible underlying motives, you generally have sufficient information to be able to evaluate the process to be expected and the underlying, often unexpressed themes.

14.4 PROCEDURAL INTERVENTIONS

Here we are concerned with planning the methods and techniques (in the broadest sense of the word) to be introduced. Among them there are both simple rules applicable to communication and group work and also refined techniques for analysis and forming judgements. The quality of a collective learning process is the result of both the content of contributions made by those involved and the way in which they work together. The function of procedures is to regulate the process of cooperation that leads to an optimum result in terms of content.

On the one hand procedures must fit in with the content-specific nature of the problem: for example, strategic problems demand different methods and techniques from organizational or operational ones. On the other hand, procedures must promote good mutual cooperation. In fact procedural interventions thus act as a *link* between content-specific and process-specific interventions.

Procedural interventions determine to a great extent the structure of the course, and a key question here is to what extent you wish to structure the course.

In our experience it is best to begin in a fairly structured way, especially with senior management. An unstructured start often falls completely outside the pattern of managers' expectations and thereby causes insecurity. And security is precisely one of the most important conditions for being able to and being allowed to confront participants with their own cooperative behaviour.

At the same time, however, providing a lot of structure contains within itself the danger that participants will see the methods and techniques not as aids offered but as prescribed methods of working, as a result of which the course acquires a prescriptive character. The structure must give a ... work to the themes approached and provide suffici... for participants to fill in this thematic frame in their ... way. Educational staff need to bring structure into the discussion as soon as possible and to subject it to collective decision-making. The more participants determine the structure themselves, the more staff are able to adopt a supporting and facilitating role, consisting of clarifying, making connections, reflecting, confronting or making suggestions.

It is a good idea for the project leader to find out in advance what sort of procedures tend to be used in the company with the sort of problems on the agenda of the course, and how effective those procedures are. If they are procedures which have become a fixed part of a prescriptive system, it is advisable to choose radically different procedures for the course, because the medium is the message.

14.5 THREE BASIC PROCESSES

As has been said, the primary function of designing a plan is above all to make an inventory of *which* possible interventions could be made *when* and *why*. It needs to be realized that three processes interlink in an organizational course and that they should be fine-tuned to each other by means of these interventions.

Firstly, there is a *decision-making process*, perhaps even several decision-making processes for organizational courses are about the collective approach to a problem or problems. In planning the decision-making process we follow the dynamics of the process. Usually it has three phases, each with different dynamics. The first phase is the period in which the participants share information. The result is a shared definition of the problem and criteria to test the solution. The second phase is the generation of alternative solutions. In the third phase the choice is made between solutions. In the first phase everybody can contribute to the process; dynamically it results in a 'we' orientation. During the second and especially the third phases, the dynamics become more complex because choices have to be made. We shall again state briefly what we understand by this.

Problem definition phase:
- Making an inventory and putting the available information in ordered form.
- Analysis of the provisional description of the problem.
- Reformulation of the problem.
- Establishing the criteria which must be fulfilled by a solution.

Alternatives generation phase:
- Development of alternative solutions.
- Evaluation of the alternatives found.
- First selection, testing alternatives against the criteria.
- Second selection.

Decision-making phase:
- Choice of the best alternative.

Described in this way, it is a prescriptive model, logical in content, which, however, under the influence of the other processes, often does not run so logically. In fact you can see a highly interactive process in which the phases interchange and influence each other; after all, decision-making is an incremental process guided by logic and interactional processes.

The second process is of course the *learning cycle*: the process of doing, reflecting, thinking and deciding. This, too, is a normative model, arising from ideas about learning. Here, too, in reality, the process does not adhere rigidly to these four phases, although at least all stages do need to be fulfilled. Even more so, for an organizational course (the start of a new way of learning) the cycle must, in our opinion, be run through several times. We shall return to this in more detail in the next section.

The third process is the process of *group development*, a process which is more easily recognizable the less one works with previously established groupings in the company. This process is achieved in four stages – in Tuckmans terms: forming, storming, norming and performing:

- *Forming*: this is the phase of seeing which way the cat jumps; testing what is and what is not allowed. It is an orientation phase in which participants get to know each other.

- *Storming*: this is the phase in which it is established who determines what and how the group is going to operate: a confrontation of wills and taking up positions. In this phase the leadership issue is dealt with; conflict in whatever form is part of this.
- *Norming*: once the question of distribution of influence has been settled, there is a basis for shared views, values, norms and rules. The atmosphere becomes relaxed and cohesion develops around the norms of the 'elite' of the group.
- *Performing*: the group is able to and does set to work. The stability of the relationship dimension allows for effective work on the task dimension.

The pace and smooth running of the other two processes are strongly influenced by this third process.

All three processes are in themselves reasonably predictable and thus form a basis for planning the interventions, but because of the interaction that occurs between the three processes, it is always uncertain what the outcome will be, and particularly *when* what will occur and therefore also when which interventions are adequate.

The Implementation Phase

> Show me how you do it, and I will tell you why
> you do it.

15.1 FIVE PHASES

Regardless of what we said in the previous chapter about the unpredictability of the collective learning and educational process, we believe there are at least five phases which must be gone through during a course intended as the first step on the road towards a learning organization. In our experience these phases are sequentially linked, each one having a definite outcome which must be achieved before there is any sense in moving on to the next. The phases are listed below:

- initial contract
- collective problem recognition
- individual problem recognition
- action planning
- follow-up contract

The initial contract phase results in an agreement between the participants themselves and between participants and educational staff to embark upon a collective learning process: '*We want to learn*'.

The phase of collective recognition and acknowledgement of the problem results in agreement on what is undesirable in the present situation and in current behaviour; on what is desired in the future situation and in future behaviour and it results in the decision to undertake to tackle this problem: '*We know what we must and want to learn and unlearn*'.

The phase of individual problem recognition and acknowledgement results in individual readiness to work on one's own behaviour and to support the collective decision to continue the learning process: *'I want to learn and unlearn'*.

The action planning phase results in a collective action plan: *'We agree on how we want to learn'*.

The phase of the follow-up contract with the instigator results in a reciprocal mandate: *'We agree on who can, is allowed to, must, wants to and will do what'*.

In each phase, decisions are made and the whole learning cycle is performed, five times in the whole programme. In this chapter we shall describe each phase in more detail, with particular emphasis on the task of the educational staff.

15.2 THE INITIAL CONTRACT

This phase coincides with the last stage of the contract phase mentioned in Chapter 13. It is a question of making a series of agreements about apparently very simple matters such as: how shall we conduct our discussions, how shall we divide up time, how can we give each other feedback and what is the role of the educational staff? It is a contract which has to be made at the doing level. In other words, each phase of the learning cycle, however short, has to be accomplished, including the participants' decision to want to take part. Demonstrating the will to do this, through actual exhibited behaviour, is of decisive importance.

It is also essential to allow sufficient time at the beginning of the programme for the accomplishment of this phase. The worst problem is often that participants from prescriptive organizations do not expect this or at any rate start out from the assumption that this kind of agreement is restricted to the level of talk theory. On the basis of their experience they associate educational courses with taking in knowledge and insights through listening or with the learning of techniques from experts. The art is to break through this non-participative attitude and make clear that the staff, their concepts, theories and techniques are not central but that what matters is what part they, the participants, actually do or do not play. Breaking through these barriers requires a reasonable level of security within the group. This phase therefore takes time.

At the same time it is a question of being accepted as staff, in the sense of helpers. They have to earn that trust through showing complete openness with respect to what has gone before, the role they adopt during the course and what they are working towards. Openness especially about how the contract with the instigators is drawn up, the extent to which staff are independent and where their independence ceases. The benefit of the doubt to be gained in this way needs to be built up by showing that the agreements made are taken extremely seriously and treated with care.

15.3 COLLECTIVE PROBLEM RECOGNITION AT THE TALK LEVEL

This phase is concerned with the collective recognition and acknowledgement of what is undesirable in the present situation and in current behaviour, and the shared definition of criteria which the desired situation and the desired behaviour would have to fulfil.

Project leaders are often confronted with two sorts of extreme attitude. The first category is from participants who seek refuge in the past or in the future. Both are worried about today and idealize what there was yesterday or what there will be tomorrow. They thereby fail to appreciate the problem of which they, in fact, form a part. The second category is formed from those who fight against the present by trying to pre-empt it, bringing forward solutions before they have really understood the problem.

The only system of avoiding always frustrating one of these two categories is to refine problem definition by means of a constant interchange of reflection and thinking with deciding and doing. Until, at least at the talk level, consensus can be reached on the situation that is undesirable at present and the one that is desired for the future. The most important task of the educational staff is to keep on consistently raising questions about the relevance of today and the future for the here and now.

Once the situation is defined in such a way that participants can change it themselves, it is normally quite easy to reach consensus on the desired situation, or at least on the desired direction for behavioural change. Shared insight and shared willingness have been achieved. We call this problem 'recognition at the talk level'. This is often the moment to start discussing procedural interventions from the staff and thereby to subject these interventions to collective decision-making.

15.4 INDIVIDUAL PROBLEM RECOGNITION AT THE ACTION LEVEL

This is the phase in which participants are called upon in any number of ways to transform talk theories into actual behaviour. This confrontation is embarrassing. It not only shows up how great the discrepancy sometimes is between, on the one hand, what is collectively understood and desired, and, on the other hand, what the individual is actually capable of. It also shows that collective action is the sum of a series of individual actions. It illustrates that collective action depends upon everyone's individual contribution to the whole. In short, everyone comes face to face with themselves.

It is, therefore, understandable that for this reason mis-apprehensions can arise in this phase: 'I did it properly, it was "them"' – 'the situation', 'the exercise' or 'the staff'. All the familiar defence mechanisms of the prescriptive organization are trotted out.

The staff (Them) run the risk in this phase of becoming the target of collective fantasies (They set us up, deliberately), and taking the blame for the participants' shortcomings.

On the one hand the educational staff must not hesitate to hold up as clear a mirror to participants as possible, however threatening this may sometimes be; and on the other hand they must not appear to 'punish' or to 'accuse', but rather to offer the security and support needed to be willing to look inquisitively into the mirror. In our experience it is often best to divide these two roles between two complementary members of staff working together.

If it goes well this phase results in the individual recognition that 'I' am part of 'the' problem, and that the problem is therefore also going to remain 'my' problem, unless 'I' play a part in solving it. This amounts to a recognition of the fact that the problem has arisen partially through 'my' dysfunctional behaviour. If you are not part of the solution you are part of the problem.

The phase ends when individuals have made the decision to contribute to the collective learning process.

The decisive factor for whether this result is achieved or not is the attitude of the hierarchically superior members of the group, the informal and formal leaders. So long as these are not prepared to discuss their own functional and especially dysfunctional contribution to the common problem – to put it simply, they keep out of range – this result will not be achieved, and neither will the goal of the course.

In this phase, the staff's task is principally a reflecting one: holding up a mirror to the participants' individual, content-specific and process-specific contributions. This mirror needs to be held up particularly and especially to the leaders. They should certainly not be spared because of their position or importance. This places high demands not only on the courage, integrity and objectivity of the course tutors, but also on the contract with the instigators.

15.5 ACTION PLANNING

There often now follows a phase of hard and enthusiastic work on collectively developing a plan of how the group intends to approach the problem, what they aim to achieve and what conditions will be necessary for it.

The staff mainly sit in the 'dugout' in this phase and restrict themselves to explaining, making suggestions or correcting.

The content of interventions is limited to occasional explanatory concepts. When necessary, procedural suggestions are made in the form of definite methods and techniques. At process level, interventions are aimed at the continued existence of distinctions such as:

- *'Me'-problems*: what is my part in the organization's problem and what should my contribution be?
- *'Us'-problems*: what is the part of those present here in the problem and our contribution to it?
- *'Them'-problems*: what are we allowed to say to others, to them, including the instigator?

In this phase it is very frequently found that 'me'-problems become 'us'-problems and 'us'-problems become 'them'-problems. Given the nature of the course the staff must principally focus on 'us'-problems.

The phase results in a decision about what is to be done by group members themselves, which matters need to be discussed with the instigator and what people want to have done by the instigator.

15.6 THE FOLLOW-UP CONTRACT

This phase is only on the agenda if the instigator is not also one of the participants of the course. At the beginning of the course a contract was concluded with the instigator, in which the latter handed over a problem to the learning group with the request to solve it or at least develop a solution for the approach to it. It is appropriate to conclude the course with a meeting, in which this initial contract is confirmed and amended and/or supplemented as necessary.

The confrontation has to fulfil at least four goals:

- Preparing for the meeting spurs participants on to use their time effectively, to fix priorities, to overcome difficulties and to take on co-responsibility. These are all essential learning points in a collective learning process.
- The way in which participants present their plans to the instigator, request the mandate to be allowed to execute their plan and state what they expect from the instigator is the first test of the newly learned behaviour in the 'real' world. Do they manage to do this in the desired, learning, adult manner?
- As such it is also a test and thus a moment of learning for the instigator, who again becomes a co-participant in the collective learning process.
- If they succeed in making good agreements, including agreements on how to ensure that they are met, then the most important step has been taken to prevent it becoming a non-participative course.

Such a meeting must therefore contain more than just a series of presentations to be heard by the instigator. Dialogue should take place and decisions be made. At the end of the meeting participants should have the courage to look back and see to what extent they realized the collectively desired behaviour. For both parties this session is 'the moment (in fact, the moments) of truth'; for the instigator at least as much as for the participants.

In this session it becomes clear whether the participants and the instigators are prepared to enter into debate with each other as adults and to make decisions about the core problem and decisions to be taken. If they succeed in achieving this goal in this session, a norm will have been set for the future.

The responsibility of the educational staff is to enable this goal and this norm to be reached; not to achieve it themselves!

15.7 RUNNING EDUCATIONAL COURSES

In Chapter 4, we defined education as carrying out interventions in a learning process. This is the prime responsibility of the staff, and it requires an accurate perception of which phase the learning process is in, at any given time. The type of intervention required and the way it should be carried out are largely dependent on which phase the learning process is in.

Educational staff, particularly the project leader, are responsible for steering the programme in such a way that all these phases are gone through and succeed each other at the appropriate time.

Perhaps the most important skill here is correct timing. The effectiveness of an intervention depends at least as much on *timing* as on quality.

Collective Learning: A Paradoxical Process

Those who understand 'it', do not speak of 'it';
those who speak of 'it', do not understand 'it'.

Adapted from: Lao Tse

16.1 VARIOUS PARADOXES

At the start of an organizational course, in the contract phase, it is explained to participants that this kind of course is not concerned with the learning of individuals, but with the learning of a collective. Indeed, staff will not be paying so much attention to what and how the individual learns as to what and how the *group* learns: to collective competence.

This is always quite difficult to explain, because here it involves a paradox. A collective can only learn by means of the individual learning of the members of that collective. If individuals do not learn, then the group will also not learn. On the other hand, however, when individuals learn, this does not necessarily mean that the group has also learned. Collective competence does not equal the sum of individual competences. A group can achieve what none of the individuals can do. But the converse also happens: a group can *fail* to achieve what any of the individuals could easily accomplish. The competence of a group is primarily determined by the way in which its members use each other's individual competences. Collective competence is determined by the interactional competence of individuals.

The second paradox is that participants of an organizational course must individually unlearn what they have learned

will and courage

obligation and
permission

knowledge and   action and ability
understanding

Figure 15 The prescriptive organization.

together as a collective. In an organizational course collectively developed rules, insights and principles will be subjected to discussion. It is this collective agreement on what is permitted and what is obligatory which dictates the knowledge and understanding, the courage, the will and the ability of a collective. In an organizational course it is precisely this collective agreement that is the subject under discussion, and with it the ability and knowledge of each individual.

An organization which seeks to change its collective behaviour must be ready to discuss what has determined its collective behaviour. This is a paradox which becomes more awkward the higher the level of learning involved. With triple loop learning, at the level of principles, the paradox implies that you should discuss what it has been agreed not to discuss.

In an organizational course, you fall back entirely upon your own individual competence, or even worse upon your own gradually emerging incompetence.

It is precisely in this kind of situation that a third paradox often manifests itself. Things are done, thought or decided upon *collectively*, which *none*, or only a small proportion, of the individuals agrees with. This is the most difficult phenomenon for the educational staff to deal with.

These phenomena also occur in individual courses, but are of no consequence there, with the result that the staff can ignore them or content themselves – as part of the course – with pointing them out. But in an organizational course it is the task of the staff to help the group through them. Only then is the group ready to move on to the next phase. In this respect a collective course is quite distinct from an individual course, and course tutors of collectives thus also differ from course tutors of individuals. One of the first reactions of a group to this paradoxical situation is collective *blindness* to the problem which gave rise to the course. This generally occurs in particular in the first phases of the course. In later phases, particularly the third phase, phenomena arise which indicate a collective *avoidance* of dealing with the problem. Throughout the whole course there is the possibility of an underlying collective *reluctance*. Even when the problem is indeed recognized and the will and courage to tackle it are present, *collective ignorance* can still lead to it not happening.

The key question for educational staff is to find out the extent to which this collective blindness, avoidance, reluctance and ignorance is the sum of individual ability, knowledge, understanding, courage and will, or is the result of a complex process in which people talk each other into things or impose upon and impute ideas to each other. A key question to which you can only get the answer by asking it *at the right moment.*

16.2 COLLECTIVE BLINDNESS

This is experienced when the group acts as if the problem which has given rise to the course simply does not exist. Blindness can occur at various levels:

- blindness to internal and external signals indicating that there is a problem;
- blindness to the fact that there is a problem which requires a solution;
- blindness to the alternative solutions which require action;
- blindness to one's own ability to carry out these solutions.

Collective blindness often arises through blindness on the part of one or more individuals. There are generally individuals to be found on every level who fail to recognize something. Whether this individual blindness will carry over into collective blindness depends largely on the influence of the individuals on the other participants. It sometimes happens, however, that (almost) all participants collectively exhibit a blind spot.

Blindness towards the existence of the collective problem, even when it occurs unconsciously, often has the function of preventing your own contribution to the problem from being subjected to discussion, and thereby avoiding the need to change your behaviour.

It is very important for the staff to adjust their interventions to suit the current level of blindness. Inappropriate interventions, such as offering alternative solutions at a time when there is no consensus over the problem, will lose their impact and there is a grave danger that they will be taken as prescriptive.

From the very beginning of the course attention needs to be paid to internal and external signals and their meaning. Only when these have been collectively recognized and acknowledged as indicating problems, can one speak of a shared problem which demands closer analysis and definition. The next question is whether the problem is considered to be solvable, or, in other words, whether the situation can be changed. When that no longer goes unrecognized, the action phase is embarked upon. Blindness of the group's own collective ability to change the situation can occur in this phase.

The different levels of blindness often manifest themselves in the different phases of the learning cycle.

Blindness to internal and external signals is principally found in the reflection phase. Indeed that is the phase in which the group looks back with detachment over collective experiences, attempting to exchange and give meaning to external signals (what we see) and internal signals (what we feel). Some participants find it difficult or even threatening to deal with feelings. We call them *emotion evaders*. Rather than taking their own feelings of unease or anger seriously, they blind themselves to these emotions out of fear that they may not be able to cope with them.

Blindness to the problem itself tends to become manifest during the thinking phase, when *thought evaders* make their appearance. They are people who find the problems awkward or, through astonishment, are not capable of analysing them and continually press for action.

Blindness to the existence of alternative solutions emerges mostly during the decision-making phase. On the one hand, it is then that those people manifest themselves who only see the 'trees'; people who pay excessive attention to detail and can always show that any solution will not work in the present situation. On the other hand, other people manifest themselves who see only the 'wood', and come up with the most all-encompassing solutions, which have little to do with the real, concrete problem.

In the doing phase, a frequent form of blindness is saying yes and then doing nothing. *Action evaders* fling themselves into drawing up even more plans from reluctance or lack of ability to go into action.

The best way for staff to prevent individual blindness from spilling over into collective blindness is to demand consideration for and give space to opposites; bring thought evaders into dialogue with action evaders, have those who only see the trees listen to those who see the wood, and vice versa. This is only possible if there is enough diversity in the group. It is then also a subject of attention in the selection phase. If the problem is mainly blindness towards external signals, a good intervention is to bring representatives from the outside world into the course: clients, consumers, financiers.

16.3 COLLECTIVE AVOIDANCE

Breaking through the above-mentioned paradoxes demands *courage*. Courage of individuals. It also requires the group to be prepared to subject agreed frameworks to discussion: what is obligatory and what is permitted. However, subjecting that collectively to discussion only takes place if individuals have summoned up the courage to break through existing rules, insights and principles. The greater the divergence between what individual participants see, feel or want, and what actually happens around them, the greater the courage required to 'come out into the open, and therefore the greater the paradox. The collective fear is that, by expressing your own opinion, you will be ridiculed, ignored or excluded. Indeed, one of the accepted ways of proving that you belong or wish to belong to a group, to the elite, is to demonstrate which subjects may or may not be spoken about; to show that you understand 'it'. By daring to discuss 'it', you merely reveal that you have not understood 'it', and jeopardize your membership of the group, 'those who understand "it" '.

At an individual level this tension is often released by manipulating your own inner views, opinions and feelings, and shaping them into outward reasons which make your behaviour seem rational. One of the commonest of such rationalizations is 'I don't want to be a spoilsport'; 'If everyone thinks or wants this, I am not going to be the one to spoil the harmony'. If several members use this rationalization, it can lead to collective decisions being taken or things being done which none of the individual members wishes. Everyone sits tight and privately disagrees with the proposal which they believe is agreed upon by the others. Because nobody is open about their real opinion, everybody has the impression that the plan, proposal or diagnosis is supported by everyone else and that the best strategy is to support it. The unconscious fear of being the 'odd man out' means that often the most ardent supporters are those most doubtful about the proposed course of action.

At group level, this tension is often released by acting out 'as if' problem-solving and thereby avoiding the consequences that go with 'real' problem solving. This 'as if' behaviour is often an unconscious process for many. Apparent solutions are found and then individuals simply act as if with these solutions the problem has been made to vanish. 'As if' problem-solving can often be recognized by its failure to take account of the time factor. It is expressed in a limited number of forms:

- fight: contesting something or someone with a vehemence that bears no relation to the influence of this factor or person on the problem;
- flight: wasting time by occupying yourself with things that are not essential for solving the problem: procedures, mutual sensitivities and so on;
- pairing: observing if an activity or a conflict between a limited number of group members will produce the solution which will remove all the problems;
- dependency: making themselves as a group dependent on 'them' and waiting for the solution to be produced entirely by someone else. 'Them' can be the board of management, clients or the educational staff.

Another way of escaping from this stress situation is collective blindness to the problem: the signals, the problem itself, or the possibilities of actually doing anything about it.

The course staff have a double task here, and it should preferably be fulfilled by two separate staff members:

- Holding up a mirror to confront participants with their 'as if' behaviour; something which can be very threatening.
- At the same time, enabling the group to discuss its mutual feelings of insecurity and fear; something which calls for protection to create enough security.

What the educational staff per se must certainly not take on is the responsibility for the group, for example by coming forward with proposals for content, plans or solutions. Nor must they succumb to 'as if' behaviour or be contaminated by feelings of fear. The paradox can often only be broken by means of an impasse, stalemate or conflict. What the staff must demonstrate above all is integrity and care. An organizational course is not inconsequential, and the fears are realistic. Indeed, at the end of the course, the group will be answerable to the instigator. It will have to show that the time spent during the week resulted in actionable steps and to demonstrate mature problem-solving oriented behaviour. On the one hand, this increases the participants' realization that they cannot allow themselves to keep on indulging in 'as if' behaviour. On the other hand, it intensifies the fear of unpredictable, unintended outcomes.

16.4 COLLECTIVE RELUCTANCE

In almost every course, there are one or two participants who consciously do not wish to take part in the learning process, either because they do not agree with the goal, or because they feel that their personal interests are jeopardized. If that comes clearly and obviously to the fore, that is no problem for the course; their behaviour does not lead to collective reluctance. It is, of course, a problem for the individuals concerned, who see themselves confronted with an important choice: to take part or not.

Collective reluctance occurs when participants come from an organization in which, for years, they have never been asked what they want, and thus they have collectively unlearned the ability to express this, something which often occurs in prescriptive organizations. When these participants are then confronted in the course, especially in the phases where decisions have to be made, with a question of will, collective insecurity occurs. An insecurity which often leads to everyone being more concerned with what the others, particularly the formal or informal leaders, want, than with what they themselves want. And so they create for themselves and each other an imagined cage based on untested 'collective' will. This collective reluctance is usually expressed by waiting for new tasks either from the staff or from the leaders of the group. If these are not forthcoming the insecurity then increases, and the tension does too, until someone breaks through the circle.

Another possibility is that the present situation, however problematical it is judged to be by the participants, still offers so many advantages to each of the individuals, that they collectively agree to have no interest in changing the situation.

Thus, individuals might be in agreement with each other that the dominant, centralistic style of management is undesirable, although collectively they maintain this system because many people individually find it is very convenient to be able to shunt responsibility upwards. Similarly, in another example, collective complaints may have been made about the lack of room for creativity and individual initiative; individuals, however, are afraid of making mistakes or taking risks.

A generally valid rule is that when participants are agreed with each other about what is undesirable in a situation and are in a position to change it, but when they none the less allow the situation to continue, collective reluctance is present. Continuing with learning and education then only has any point if people clearly let each other know what everyone's interest is in maintaining the status quo, and they are prepared to negotiate on the conditions under which they are prepared to relinquish this interest.

16.5 COLLECTIVE IGNORANCE

Collective ignorance arises when a group has the courage and the will to approach the problem, but lacks knowledge in terms of either content or process. If it is based on a lack of content-specific knowledge, that is seldom a problem. That can usually be fixed with a short presentation, with literature or some other method without any problem. Ignorance at process level is much more difficult to handle, being an ignorance which particularly manifests itself in an awkward way of communicating.

Especially in prescriptive organizations, 'passing the buck' is a favourite game. Unanimity and harmony are also important norms in this type of organization. Conflicts must be avoided. Contradictions inherent in the system have taught people to communicate *indirectly* a great deal. The most penetrating signal for this is the frequent misuse of the words 'them' and 'us'. This kind of collectively, and largely unconsciously learned, indirect communication can render a group completely incapable of approaching a problem, even if the insight, the will and the courage are present.

The goal of communication is to transmit an intention to another person and thereby to obtain an effect on the other person. In the process, two types of translation take place. The sender translates intention into behaviour: a word or a deed. The recipient translates, or interprets, this behaviour into an effect. During this translation process mistakes can occur on either side, with the consequence that the effect the sender obtains differs from the original intention.

The two basic errors in communication which are encountered very frequently are that the *sender* identifies with the recipient *too much*, or the *recipient* identifies with the sender *too little*.

The sender's excessive identification with the other person leads to what we call 'stratego-thinking'. At the start of the board-game 'Stratego', it is important to place the pieces well. Most people expect the bombs around the target, the flag. Because everybody knows this, opponents can be surprised by placing the bombs elsewhere; but everybody knows this, too, so the flag can be placed somewhere different, as well. A crafty player anticipates this and so the game goes on. In stratego-thinking you are influenced in what you want to say or do more by what you think the other person is thinking and wants to hear, than by what you yourself think and feel. The individual position thus degenerates into a compromise between what you really think and what you think will be acceptable to the other person. From the very beginning of the interaction chain the communication is thus clouded. The recipient reacts again to this compromise by taking account of what the speaker has just said. The consequence of stratego-thinking is that it becomes less and less clear who exactly thinks what. Mutual communication drifts further and further away from the individual position and floats away. Often stratego-thinking even goes so far that people start to speak on behalf of someone else, or even on behalf of the whole group.

Conversely, the recipient identifies too little with the sender. Instead of listening from within the reference framework to the opinions and values of the sender and if necessary asking exactly what the latter means, the recipient begins to guess at the intentions behind the behaviour, on the basis of their own opinions and values. In an organization where looking for scapegoats is a popular pastime, negative intentions are often assumed to underlie behaviour, with the result that solely through the poor manner of communication a general feeling of distrust can arise, which was exactly what this sophisticated way of communicating was supposed to prevent, and thus, we find ourselves faced with a self-fulfilling prophecy.

It is a good idea for educational staff to introduce rules for successful communication at the start of the course, and then to intervene regularly on the basis of these agreed rules. At critical moments, it is important to give participants insight into the interaction which is taking place. Many people think of communication in terms of cause and effect (*linear causality*). They explain their own behaviour as a reaction to what others do, without grasping the fact that the others are reacting to what they do. They fail to understand the *circular causality* of communication.

Furthermore, people react more strongly to what others *do* than to what they say, particularly if there is a conflict between saying and doing. It is essential for staff to be clear and direct in their way of communicating, to say what they think and, above all, to do what they say.

Good role-model behaviour is by far the most significant medium available to the educational staff.

Figure 16 The learning organization.

16.6 THE CENTRAL QUESTION: WHAT DO WE WANT?

In Section 16.1 we depicted an organization as a triangle with permission and obligation in the centre. This is the dominant feature of a prescriptive organization. However, in an organizational course, permission and obligation are the actual subject matter for discussion, the key to what holds the group together. The most significant learning is in discovering, collectively, a new point of reference in the collective will. The dominant feature of a learning organization is its focus on learning, based on its collectively shared will.

The Role of the Educational Staff: Educating or Advising?

If you give somebody advice which he does not
follow, he will immediately blame it.
If you give him advice which he does take,
he will only blame you later on.

Maurice Domay

There is a good chance that amongst the organizational
consultants who have read this part of the book some (but not
all and not even the majority) will say that the activities
described in it have nothing to do with education but with
advising. They might be right, but the question still arises as to
what the real difference is between this form of education and
certain forms of advising.

Organizational courses, as described here, originated from the
management in-company courses such as came into fashion in
the 1980s. They were thus developed by the educational
profession, and also described by us, who contributed to their
development for ten years, from the point of view of educators.
That profession is concerned with helping to learn. The
collective aspect is new in this concept of helping organizations
to learn. The inclusion of reflection and particularly of decision-
making, as essential components of a learning process, is also
new.

For many organizational consultants, there is nothing new in
all of this. On the contrary, they specialize in helping
organizations, or collectives, to make decisions. The new idea
for organizational consultants is that decision-making is part of

learning, and that a process of organizational change is a learning process. As such, it is a process which requires help; that help is called education.

Also in the 1980s, consultants emerged, who applied themselves more and more to linking directly educational activities and consultancy work. If these advisers were to write a book about the activities we describe in this part, they would perhaps not call such activities educating, and they would emphasize different aspects. However, they would ultimately be describing the same phenomena. Both are concerned with a new form of help towards organizational change, and possibly with a *new profession*.

The essential feature of a prescriptive organization is that in these organizations the process of organizational change is detached from the resulting process of behavioural change. This dichotomy explains why, in the postwar years, organizational consulting companies have segregated their educational activities, accommodating them in separate institutions.

The essence of a learning organization is, by contrast, that the process of organizational change coincides with the process of behavioural change. They are one and the same process. The management of organizational change processes is, within a learning organization, the leading of a collective learning process. Assistance with these processes is an area in which advising and education coincide and therefore so do the professions of consultant and educator.

One theme that has preoccupied organizational consultants for decades concerns the following two questions:

- Which role should the consultant play? In simple terms, there is a choice between the expert role and the support role.
- What should the consultant concentrate on? In simple terms, he can concentrate on content (the what) and process (the how).

Here the supporting role often coincides with a focus on process consultation and the expert role with a focus on content. This is where the distinction arose between the content expert – the *solution provider* – and the process consultant – the *problem clarifier*.

In 1972, Zwart tackled this contrast in a extremely polite if not euphemistic manner, and came up with an alternative in which the distinction is no longer relevant. Or, to put it differently, one in which the consultant must be able to be an expert as well as providing support and be able to deal with both content and process. He called that the *learning model*!

Even at that time, Zwart could see that changing is synonymous with learning and that the art of consultancy is helping an organization to 'learn how to learn'. It is no more than *helping*, but also, no less. We quote: 'He (i.e. the consultant) will have to come to terms with the fact that the less he is prepared to appeal to the client's adult judgement potential, the less effective his help will ultimately be. The dynamics of a process of change are linked to the client's readiness and ability to learn how to learn.' That is the role of the consultant; the same is true, *mutatis mutandis*, for the educator. Almost twenty years later, by a long and circuitous route, we ultimately come to the same conclusion, but with the important addition that it is a matter of (helping) the learning of a collective, and that is essentially something quite different from (helping) the learning of (a group of) individuals.

If consulting and educating are seen as synonymous with helping to learn, yet another choice must be faced when it comes to role conceptions: a choice which can be applied equally to consultants or to educators. Namely, between being willing or unwilling to acknowledge, not just verbally, but in attitude and behaviour, the client's *ability to form adult judgements*, and the resultant role of the consultant or the educator, namely that of helper. This choice coincides with the dominant distinction made throughout this book between learning and prescriptive approaches.

The Learning Organization: Fashion or Necessity?

In the twentieth century, in the space of less than one hundred years the western world has succeeded in developing a form of organization which has brought with it an unprecedented degree of affluence, both in scope and in range. An organizational structure which more than ever before has created job security for people and offered access to an unheard-of choice of products and services than at any other time. An organization based on two essential basic principles: *efficiency* and *justice*. It is called *bureaucracy*.

Now, at the end of the twentieth century, bureaucracy faces the same dilemma suffered millions of years ago by the dinosaur: how to avoid extinction through lack of adaptability.

The survival of bureaucracy is threatened by its own success. The revolutionary technological developments set in motion not least by the bureaucracies themselves, create in the environment in which they operate such a dynamic that the bureaucracies are themselves confronted with their basic weakness: the inability to adapt from within, to *develop*.

Bureaucracies have landed in the vicious, self-reinforcing circle of a prescriptive system; a cooperative association between people which, in the course of time, becomes subject to its own regularities that can no longer be influenced by people. Furthermore the system reinforces itself in its features because it is not a learning system but a prescriptive one. The system takes care of its people, but with the result that the people begin to take less and less care of the system. This is a system-intensifying process because bureaucracy attracts the very people who wish to be cared for instead of looking after themselves and the system.

The question arises of why this system becomes stronger and stronger. What would need to be changed in the system so that it could be transformed into a structure created by people themselves? In our opinion it is the hierarchical stratification of the system, in which thinking, deciding, reflecting and doing are separated from each other. However, this distinction is far older than the system. It is rooted in a centuries old ordering of our society.

The Origins of Present-day Working Organizations:
Church and Army

Bureaucracies are organizations in which the ordering of people is a central feature. At the top sit people who, by virtue of their greater perspective of the situation, their experience and wisdom are competent and therefore entitled to give leadership. At the bottom are the subordinates who are considered to be loyal implementers of the decisions made at the top.

Present-day working organizations have evolved from around the second half of the nineteenth century, when the only experience of large-scale, working organizations was derived from the Church and the Army. To a large extent, they have also acted as models for contemporary companies.

In the Churches, the difference between hierarchical levels is determined by differences in knowledge that the people have of the faith and its values and especially differences in devotion exhibited. Moving up to a higher level is coupled with an initiation which is the result of and results in a higher level of grace. In the Army there is also a strong hierarchy based on experience, knowledge and loyalty, and here too the transition to a higher rank is associated with initiation rituals.

The loftiest echelons of both organizations are reserved for the highest social classes. In both Church and Army, there is a hierarchical ordering of people who differ qualitatively from each other. A difference which is a reflection of the social order which is again in its turn seen as a reflection of the celestial order.

In 595, Pope Gregory the Great wrote a letter to his bishops informing them why they were to acknowledge the primacy of the Bishop of Arles: 'The example of the heavenly hosts teaches us that God's creatures cannot be governed if all are equal to each other: there are angels and archangels, who are clearly not equal to each other, they differ in both power and rank' (Duby,1978). The heavenly order is actually even more complicated. In heaven there are nine sorts of angels: seraphims, cherubims, thrones, dominations, strengths, powers, principalities and then archangels and angels. This knowledge of the Church of the celestial order gives it the right to intervene in the social order because it is in 'that transitory state which is wresting mankind slowly away from its roots in time and space. The angels give God-like enlightenment throughout the world to the bishops for the revelation of the Earthly hierarchies.' The bishops have the obligation and the privilege of testing the earthly order against that of heaven. This accounts for the mediaeval legitimization of feudalism. The order of human social life must mirror the perfection of the heavenly order. In its turn, organizational order mirrors social order. Why else would so many contemporary bureaucracies have nine hierarchical levels?

Church and Army espouse a feudal model in which the lower levels exchange *loyalty* and *discipline* for security. In the feudal way of life respect for differences in position is essential. Individuals earn (self) respect by knowing their place and contributing to the community on that basis. Loss of face is also something to be avoided at all costs. The preservation of mutual relationships and the maintenance of formal harmony is of great importance, and if everyone abides by the rules, mutual harmony will not be disrupted. Conflicts which do not become public leave formal harmony intact. If a conflict is swept under the table, it requires no open reaction and no harm is done. Church and Army are pre-eminently organizations directed towards the acquisition and maintenance of loyalty and discipline to the 'doctrine', but above all to the individuals who are the personification of it. Loyalty to these persons creates security.

In both Church and Army, establishing policy is reserved for the higher ranks who have the exclusive right to make decisions. Putting them into action is left to the lower orders. Thinking and doing are kept separate. This distinction necessitates a third category of people to ensure that the directives from 'on high' are understood and carried out.

Suspicion is a legitimate attitude when it comes to relations *between* the ranks or levels in organizations. The base is controlled by a hierarchy of supervisors, who themselves obey strictly the directives from the top.

The Church and the Army are pre-eminently 'people organizations', aimed at *organizing people*. They contrast with 'working organizations' which are aimed at a good execution of *working processes*.

The Rise of Present-day Working Organizations
The large-scale working organizations arose at the time of the Industrial Revolution. Unskilled labourers migrated en masse to the cities seeking work in factories, which were organized very much along the lines on which the Church and Army were previously organized. The ideas of 'scientific management' gave legitimization to this order since rationalization of the work task led to a reduction of activities to the smallest possible unit and thus the greatest possible *efficiency*. The result was a strong centralization of decision-making and the rise of a large middle management supervising the execution.

Middle management is an illustration of the hierarchical order of people. 'Span of control' is a consequence of the fact that the boss had only limited power to supervise the implementation of the rules of play. Organizational rules are the guardians of the relationship between hierarchical levels. A well-known example is the so-called chain of command which prevents the missing out of any of the levels in vertical communication, an error which is significantly known as 'short-circuiting'; that business is also *done* is less important than that a level is bypassed.

The currents in the wake of scientific management had a corrective effect on the whole picture. Weber and his followers restricted the arbitrary power at the top with the introduction of rational criteria of justice. The human relations movement focused attention on psychological aspects which helped to determine efficiency. However, the hierarchical principles of the system remained intact. Decision-making remained the preserve of the few at the top, with action falling to the rank and file. Differences of opinion were only relevant at the top, and could only be discussed there. Outside the elevated 'inner circle', the appearance of unanimity and agreement was kept up. In dealings with the labour force the 'top' was unified and as such strongly dominant. Their dominance, orientated towards *power* and *harmony* and based on the distinction between thinking and deciding on the one hand and action on the other, laid the foundations for the prescriptive character of modern organizations.

The social and economic situation of the 1950s and 1960s created the ideal context for the development and refinement of these organizations. The social order in the Netherlands was still largely pillarized, with strong divisions between the pillars at the bottom. Coordination took place at the top, through an elite. Within the pillar there was an important difference between the 'elite' and the rank and file. Markets were sellers' markets, adapting to what was produced by industry rather than vice versa. Organizations were largely independent of their environment and were able to devote themselves to dominance, order and power. The model for these organizations was the machine: a whole composed of cogs where every cog has its own place in the whole.

The Turning of the Tide

Towards the end of the 1960s, this picture began to change. Markets became more complex, customers much more demanding and employees more vocal. Organizations applied themselves to optimizing the balance between supply and demand. Sales were no longer sufficient. Marketing and strategy began to gain ground as more comprehensive concepts. Defining the 'business', developing a recognizable 'image' and a competitive advantage were now of prime importance.

The organization was seen as a number of subsystems which together formed a whole. Interaction with the environment became essential for survival. Greater recognition and acknowledgement were given to interdependencies. The boundaries of the organization became less absolute. It began to be realized that organizations could and must reduce insecurities in the environment by entering into associations with other organizations and with political and social forces. Strategy gained great attention. The dominant theme was *adaptation*: the realization of a good 'fit' between environment and organization.

In the 1980s this was supplemented by much greater attention to *operations*. Whether we now talk of customer or market orientation, integral quality or logistics, these are still activities which intensify connections between and agreements within the *working process*. The concept of *value chain* and the critical examination of every subsection for added value in this chain is an indication of this. As a result relationships within organizations have come under increasing pressure. Competition is forcing organizations to improve coordination between departments. Survival requirement number one for an organization is a well-organized *operational core*. It is pressure from outside which is causing the internal empires, which departments so often are, to totter. Perhaps the greatest impetus to this is the tremendously fast-increasing information technology.

However, in spite of these developments the traditional view of organizations as primarily imposing order on people continues to prevail. This can be seen from the way in which people try to give these developments organizational form. Examples of this are:

- The development, during the 1970s, of structures such as work consultation and works councils, were only partly linked to the operations. They were predominantly linked and integrated with the decision-making hierarchy. This prevented the principles on which the hierarchy was based from being subjected to discussion.
- The need for developing strategy was responded to by setting up special staff departments, firmly fixed at the top. This is a typical 'mechanistic solution' for an organization which operates as an organism at 'talk level', but at the 'level of action' operates as a machine.
- Increased attention to quality resulted in the appointment of special quality managers who, however, soon took on the role of institutionalized scapegoats who could be blamed for any deficiency of quality.
- The introduction of goal-setting within an organization and per organizational unit after an analysis of responsibilities results in an intensification of the orientation towards bureaucratic boundaries in the organization.

This at a time when the problems faced by the organization really require a softening of horizontal relationships.

At the level of talk theory dialogue is very much the trend, but on the action level nothing has changed.

What we see is that organizations are frantically searching for more and more new management concepts and are always coming to the conclusion that these do not work, with the result that they go looking for the next wonder cure: portfolio management, MBWA, competitor analyses, value-chain analyses, privatization, decentralization, quality and result accountability. Why are they often so ineffective?

New Principles of Organization

Ineffectiveness will remain as long as people keep on trying to arrange organizations on the basis of classical principles. In other words, if learning and changing are only limited at the most to double loop learning. What is at stake is the classical organizing principle. In the 1980s, developments occurred which compelled the classical bureaucracies to make the transformation to triple loop learning. In our opinion three developments are decisive here, developments which are a direct consequence of the arrival of the information era.

Firstly, the 1980s witnessed a marked separation between what happens *inside* organizations and what happens *outside* and *between* organizations. The dominant mechanism controlling what happens inside organizations is the *hierarchy*. It is a means of organizing people in their roles as employees; a means of maintaining order, harmony, stability, solidarity, security and justice. It operates with vertical 'status' differences, and is primarily aimed at regulating *social* relationships.

The dominant mechanism for controlling activities outside the organizations, between one organization and another and between organizations and customers, is the *market*. The market is directed primarily towards the *regulation of business relationships*. It is a mechanism which undermines vertical status differences, disrupts harmony, stimulates the rise of self-interest and constantly threatens to cause discontinuity.

Over the last few decades outside and inside have been growing closer and closer together. *Outside*, in the market, we see increasing connections arising between organizations in the form of mergers, alliances, joint ventures, franchises, covenants and partnerships. In short, networks are developing in which both business and social relationships are regulated on the basis of equality.

Within organizations, exactly the opposite developments are taking place. Through the introduction of things like unit management, results accountability, internal budgeting and decentralization, the market is becoming a mechanism of control within organizations. Employees are spoken to about obtaining efficiency, successful negotiation and the possibilities of their own influence.

A second fundamental development, which is also largely connected with or even caused by the use of information technology, is the disappearance of the class or status society, and as a result has generated a trend known widely as *individualization*. Postconsumer society has produced a new generation: those of the age of the ego. A generation which, as far as opinion is concerned, uses notions such as: standing up for yourself, self-development and personal responsibility. A generation which judges the hierarchy by the contribution, the added value it gives to the working process, instead of the position it represents. A generation which in its mutual horizontal and vertical relationships starts out from equality and at the same time accepts and values differences. In short, an *adult* generation which respects other people's ability to make judgements and decisions.

A third essential development is the *constantly increasing pace* with which these changes are progressing. A development which is also a feature of the age of information. The life cycles of products and the time taken to develop them are getting shorter all the time. Within a few years, new technologies are again overtaken; periods of return on investment often last no longer than three years. In short, pace has become a decisive criterion of success. *Time* has become the scarcest commodity of all.

These three developments in particular, then, put at risk the traditional bases of classical, hierarchical human organization. This compels bureaucracies to convert from *organizing people* towards *organizing cooperative processes*.

From	Towards
hierarchy	markets and networks
collectivity	individualism
vertical division	mutual equivalence
horizontal equality	mutual difference
harmony	oppositions
stability	change
structure	flexibility
position and title	individually meaningful contribution
final responsibility	personal responsibility
horizontal differentiation	horizontal collaboration
efficiency	effectiveness
explanation	discovery
waiting	individual initiative
separation of thinking and doing	integration of thinking and doing
prescriptive learning	learning to learn

Table 4 Towards a new type of organization.

In this we see a horizontal and a vertical organization, with *horizontal* organization no longer predominantly based upon divisions according to homogeneity of work, or upon functional organization, but on a grouping around required achievements, relating to the product or the customer. It is a market-oriented organization, regulated and controlled to a large extent by the principles of the *market.*

Vertical organization is not primarily concerned with regulating who is whose boss, or who reports to whom, but is based on the question of which interdependencies, between which individuals and groups need to be managed. This vertical organization will, just like horizontal organization, be assessed in terms of the added value it contributes to the value chain. Many hierarchical levels will doubtless be dispensed with as a result of this assessment.

In this organizing of collaborative processes, thinking, deciding, doing and reflecting will no longer be separate, but will be integrated. In short, an organization will induce learning at all levels and by all groups, which above all will induce continuous learning, for there will be no time for keeping thinking and doing apart.

Thus we see the first contours of a new type of organization emerging, a type of organization with a wholly different emphasis from the traditional organization. In Table 4, the shift of emphasis from traditional to new organization is represented by key concepts. It is a shift which will be permanent, for in no sense does it reflect a fad of fashion. The developments unfolding around us are more complex and richer than we describe. The transformation of bureaucracies is also a considerably more complicated process than the mere modification of organizational principles. The number of aspects which are subject to change is legion. However, more significant than the individual aspects – the trees – is the mutual connection – the wood. That wood, the organization of the future, is in our opinion best represented as an organization built upon the operational core with people organized according to the added value they bring to the realization of the working process. It is an organization built around *cooperative processes,* in which people learn through cooperation and cooperate while learning: *a learning organization.*

Bibliography

Ansoff, H. Igor, *Implanting Strategic Management*. Prentice Hall, London, 1984.

Argyris, C. and Donald Schön, *Organizational Learning*. Addison-Wesley, London, 1978.

Argyris, C., *Strategy, Change and Defensive Routines*. Harvard University, Pitman Publishing, Boston, 1985.

Ashby, W.R., *An Introduction to Cybernetics*. Chapman and Hall, 1956.

Bahlmann, J.P and B.A.C. Meesters, *Denken & Doen*. Eburon, Delft, 1988.

Beer, Stafford, *The Heart of Enterprise*. John Wiley & Sons, Chichester, 1979.

Beer, Stafford, *Diagnosing the System*. John Wiley & Sons, Chichester, 1985.

Berne, E., *Games People Play*. Castle Books, New Jersey, 1964.

Bion, W., *Experiences in Groups*. Tavistock, London, 1959.

Boisot, Max, *Information & Organizations*. Fontana, London, 1987.

Bomers, Gerard, *De lerende Organisatie*. Nijenrode, September 1989.

Bos, A.H., *Oordeelsvorming in Groepen*. H. Veenman & Zonen BV, Wageningen, 1974.

Checkland, Peter, *Systems Thinking, Systems Practice*. John Wiley & Sons, Chichester, 1981.

Dee, G.A. van, J.W. Ganzevoort and D. Sonnefield, Management-opleidingen, liever maatwerk dan confectie. In *Intermediair*, 26-27 June, 1980.

Dijk van, Jules, *Organisatie in verandering*. Universitaire Pers Rotterdam, 1974.

Duby, Georges, *De Drie Orden*. Elsevier, Amsterdam, 1978.

Garratt, Bob, *The Learning Organization*. Fontana Paperbacks, London 1987.

Geertz, Clifford, *The Interpretation of Cultures*. Basic Books, New York, 1973.

Hall, E.T., *The Silent Language*. Doubleday & Company, New York, 1959.

Handy, Charles, *Understanding Organization*. Penguin Books, Middlesex, 1979.

Harvey, Jerry B., *The Abilene Paradox*. Lexington Books, Lexington, 1988.

Hasper, W.J.J., *De onderneming als individualiteit; op weg naar een nieuwe toekomst*. Samsom/NIVE, Alphen a/d Rijn, 1988.

Hersey & Blanchard, *Management of Organizational Behaviour, Utilizing Human Resources*, 5th ed., Prentice Hall, 1988.

Jaques, Elliott, *Requisite Organization*. Cason Hall, Arlington, 1989.

James, M. & Dorothy Jongeward, *Born to Win: Transactional Analysis with Gestalt Experiments*. Addison-Wesley, Reading MA, 1971.

Janis, Irving L. & Leon Mann, *Decision Making*. The Free Press, New York, 1977.

Kanter, R.M., *When Giants Learn to Dance*. Simon & Schuster, New York, 1989.

Kolb, D.A., Management and the Learning Process. *California Mngt Rev.*, Spring 1976, **18** (3)

Kolb D.A., *Experiential Learning*. Prentice Hall, Englewood Cliffs, 1984.

Kouwenhoven, M., (red.) *Transaktionele Analyse in Nederland*. Algemeen Nederlands Instituut voor Transaktionele Analyse, Ermelo, 1983.

Lievegoed, B.C.J., *Organiseties in Ontwikkeling: Zicht op de Toekomst*. Lemniscaat, Rotterdam, 1984.

McCall jr., Morgan W. & Robert E. Kaplan, *Whatever It Takes*. Prentice Hall, Englewood Cliffs, 1985.

Mills, Th.M., *Sociology of Small Groups*. Prentice Hall, Englewood Cliffs, 1984.

Mintzberg, Henry, *The Structuring of Organizations*. Prentice Hall, Englewood Cliffs, 1979.

Morgan, Gareth, *Images of Organization*, Sage Publications, Beverly Hills, 1986.

Nadler, D.A. and M. Tushman, Organizing for Innovation. *California Management Review*, 1986, **28** (3), 74–92.

Perrow, Charles, *Organizational Analysis*. Wadsworth Publishing Co., California, 1970.

Peters, T.J. & Waterman, R.H., *In Search of Excellence: Lessons From America's Best Run Companies*. Harper & Row, London, 1982.

Pfeffer, Jeffrey, *Organizations and Organization Theory*. Pitman, Boston, 1982.

Schein, Edgar H., *Organizational Culture and Leadership*. Jossey-Bass, San Francisco, 1985.

Thompson, J.D., *Organizations in Action*. McGraw-Hill, New York, 1967.

Toffler, A., *The Third Wave*. Pan Books, London, 1981.

Vansina, L., *Van management van veranderingen naar management van ontwikkelingen*. Intern document IOD, Leuven, February 1986.

Vansina, L., Reorganiseren onder ongunstige economische omstandigheden. In *Economisch en Sociaal Tijdschrift*, jaargang 82 nr. 1:deel I, nr. 3: deel II.

Watzlawick, P., Beavin, J.H. & Jackson, D.D., *Pragmatics of Human Communication*. W.W. Norton & Co, New York, 1967.

Weick, K.E., *The Social Psychology of Organizing*. Addison-Wesley, London, 1979.

Zuyderhoudt, R.W.L., Synergetica. In M & O, *Tijdschrift voor organisatiekunde en social beleid*, March/April, 1985.

Zwart, C.J., *Gericht Veranderen van Organisaties*. Lemniscaat, Rotterdam, 1977.

Index